Being the Parent YOU Want to Be
Facilitator Guide

12 Communication Skills
for Effective Parenting

by
Gary Screaton Page, M.Ed.,
Carol Ann Weir

Performance Learning Systems
Nevada City, California

Performance Learning Systems, Publishing Division, Nevada City, CA 95959
© 2000, Performance Learning Systems, Inc.
All rights reserved. Published 2000
Printed in the United States of America
10 9 8 7 6 5 4 3 2 1

Cover Design: Brook Design Group
Interior Design: Donna Burke
Editor: Barbara Brown

PLS Bookstore
224 Church Street
Nevada City, CA 95959
www.plsbookstore.com
www.plsweb.com
info@plsbookstore.com
800-506-9996

This book may be ordered from the PLS Bookstore, 224 Church Street, Nevada City, CA 95959, 800-506-9996 as well as the text it accompanies, *Being the Parent YOU Want to Be: 12 Communication Skills for Effective Parenting*. Quantity discounts are available for bulk purchases, sales promotions, premiums, fund-raising, and educational needs.

CONTENTS

INTRODUCTION

All children and their caregivers — parents, teachers, foster parents, grandparents, child care workers, and others — have the right to healthy, supportive relationships. Positive communication is part of a healthy, satisfying relationship. Good communication is not necessarily a skill we are each born with, however. We often need training to improve our communication abilities.

The book *Being the Parent YOU Want to Be: 12 Communication Skills for Effective Parenting* was written so that caregivers would have a simple and effective system for learning good communication skills. The 12 communication skills in this book have been taught to teachers with great success for over 30 years. Many teachers took the skills home and used them with their own children. They recommended that the skills be made available to parents and others who take care of children so that they, too, could improve their adult-child relationships.

Being the Parent YOU Want to Be Facilitator Guide: 12 Communication Skills for Effective Parenting was written as a companion to *Being the Parent YOU Want to Be* to provide an opportunity for parents and other caregivers to review and practice the 12 communication skills in a four-session workshop. This book presents a comprehensive, step-by-step guideline and supporting materials for those who wish to facilitate such a workshop.

HOW TO USE THIS GUIDE

THE PROGRAM

This guide provides instructions for facilitating a four-session workshop on the 12 communication skills presented in the text *Being the Parent YOU Want to Be: 12 Communication Skills for Effective Parenting*. Each session focuses on one section of the text and allows time to review and discuss the reading as well as time to practice and role-play.

The text is to be read outside of the sessions and the readings discussed within each session. (Pages 30 to 32 in the Appendix, which may be photocopied for each group member, gives instructions for the reading assignments.) Time for role-playing practice is provided in sessions 2, 3, and 4.

OVERVIEW

Any group of parents, teachers, or others involved in child care wishing to work together to learn the skills of *Being the Parent YOU Want to Be: 12 Communication Skills for Effective Parenting* is encouraged to do so. Such groups need a facilitator.

Anyone — parents, teachers, social workers, clergy, counselors, Sunday school teachers, PTA members, or others — wishing to lead such a study group may organize a workshop. It is helpful if he or she has had training in the facilitation of small groups, but it is not required.

The facilitator organizes the sessions, leads discussions, and makes sure participants have an opportunity to share their experiences, ask questions, and generally feel they are important members of the group. To be effective, the facilitator should accomplish the following tasks before the first workshop session:

- Read the book and be familiar with and comfortable using the skills.
- Complete all the activities and role-plays in *Being the Parent YOU Want to Be*.
- Read and understand the procedures in this *Facilitator Guide*.
- Learn the names of all the skills, their purposes, and how to implement them.

Note: Under no circumstances should any individual, group, or organization promote itself in any way as representing or being certified by Performance Learning Systems, Inc., the publishers of Being the Parent YOU Want to Be: 12 Communication Skills for Effective Parenting, or its author, Gary Screaton Page, M.Ed., without express permission to do so.

REPRODUCIBLE PAGES

Many reproducible pages are provided in the Appendix of this guide. Especially important are the pages that provide the outside reading assignments for the four sessions. You will find them in the Appendix on pages 30 to 32 You will also find masters from which you may make overhead transparencies or handouts of the course skills, the work sheets found in *Being the Parent YOU Want to Be* and other useful information. The pages in the Appendix are perforated near the binding to make it easy for you to remove and reproduce them.

SCHEDULING

The study of ***Being the Parent YOU Want to Be: 12 Communication Skills for Effective Parenting*** can be completed in four 2½-hour sessions, assuming participants read sections of the book before each session. Following is a schedule for the sessions:

Session No. 1:   Getting Acquainted & Part 1 "My Way, Your Way, or Our Way?" — Discovering Your Parenting Style.

Session No. 2:   Part 2 "What Are You Thinking?" — Discovering What's On Your Child's Mind.

Session No. 3:   Part 3 "I Don't Want To!" — Overcoming Your Child's Objections.

Session No. 4:   Part 4 "What WILL We Do?" — Solving Problems and Making Decisions With Your Child, Part 6 "Put It All Together," and Concluding Activities.

Note: The role-plays in Part 5 are integrated into Sessions 2, 3, and 4.

At least one week before the first session, participants should receive their personal copies of *Being the Parent YOU Want to Be: 12 Communication Skills for Effective Parenting*. Order the texts through the PLS Bookstore at 800-506-9996. When you deliver participants their copies of the text, give them instructions on how to contact you should they need to do so. Also instruct them regarding meeting times, place, and dates, and inform them of the required reading for the first session: Foreword, Introduction, and all of Part 1: "My Way, Your Way, or Our Way?" Discover Your Parenting Style. Let them know that you will assign additional reading homework at the end of each subsequent session.

You will find a sample introductory letter to participants on page 29 in the Appendix and the Reading Assignments on pages 30 to 32. Feel free to photocopy these pages for your use.

We recommend that you hold sessions at least one week apart and no less often than once a month. Doing so will give every participant enough time to read the appropriate chapter(s) and try out the skills before each meeting. Moreover, participants will come to each session with a greater number of experiences to share and issues to discuss. We highly recommend that you not try to cover all the skills in a one-day workshop for these reasons.

GENERAL PROGRAM GUIDELINES

FIND A MEETING PLACE

Find a suitable place to meet. Libraries, classrooms, restaurant or hotel group rooms, churches, or even homes all make good places to meet. Be sure to confirm the availability of the meeting place a few days before your first meeting and each subsequent session.

PURCHASE TEXTS AND MAKE READING ASSIGNMENTS

Purchase copies of *Being the Parent YOU Want to Be* for your workshop participants (plus several extra), or ask your participants to purchase the texts on their own. (See page 81 in the back of this guide for ordering information.) Be sure participants receive their texts well before the first meeting to have time to read the first assignment and fill out the required worksheets. Parents and teachers are busy people and will need at least a week to do the first assignment.

On pages 30 through 32 in the Appendix, you will find masters for your pages that detail the reading assignments. You may tear the masters out of this book and photocopy them. Be sure participants receive their assignments and their texts at the same time.

REMIND GROUP MEMBERS ABOUT THE MEETING

Remind group members of their reading assignment, the meeting location, and time. People are busy and a reminder is often welcome. You might call or email each of them a day ahead. Especially remind them to bring their copies of *Being the Parent YOU Want to Be* to each session!

PROVIDE REFRESHMENTS

You may wish to provide refreshments or have group members contribute. The availability of refreshments often helps people feel more comfortable and relaxed. If you decide to have refreshments, gather the necessary equipment to make and serve drinks and food.

CHECK YOUR EQUIPMENT NEEDS

You will need:

☐ Copies of *Being the Parent YOU Want to Be* for each person. You may want to have extra copies on hand in case someone comes to a session without his or her text. These books can be ordered through the PLS Bookstore at 800-506-9996 or at www.plsbookstore.com. If you want a discount, it is best to call. Ask about group discounts if you order over 15 copies.

☐ One copy of this Facilitator Guide, which can also be ordered from the PLS Bookstore.

☐ Tables (optional if people can write in their laps).

☐ Chairs.

☐ Overhead projector, flip chart and paper, or equipment for a Microsoft PowerPoint® presentation.

☐ Transparencies (which you make from masters at the back of this book) or copies of the verbiage on the masters preprinted on flip chart paper, duplicated as handouts, or prepared as a Microsoft PowerPoint® presentation.

☐ Flip chart paper or a chalk/white board. Markers or chalk for your own use.

☐ Items for serving refreshments, such as a coffeepot, cups, plates, ice chest and ice, tableware, and napkins.

☐ Refreshments.

☐ Pencils or pens.

☐ Note paper or pads.

START ON TIME

It is highly recommended that you start on time. Avoid allowing meetings to start late. If you begin on time, people inclined to be late will make more of an effort to arrive on time at subsequent sessions.

If weather is too inclement for safe travel, cancel the meeting. At the first meeting, come to an agreement with all members about such a contingency.

PREPARE AHEAD

Read *Being the Parent YOU Want to Be* and this guide. Then read them again. A good facilitator will be aware of the organization of the text and the layout of each session. Understand and practice all 12 skills with children. Collect anecdotes from your experience for each of the skills. To get the ball rolling, have questions and topics for discussion clearly in mind.

Make transparencies using the masters in the Appendix on pages 39 through 79. Or, if you don't wish to use an overhead projector (or don't have one available to you), you may copy each master onto flip chart paper, or into a Microsoft PowerPoint® presentation, or photocopy them for handouts.

BEGIN THE FIRST SESSION

A good way to begin the first session is to ask members of the group to take turns introducing themselves and relating experiences they've had with the book so far. Perhaps they already have questions they want to raise based on the initial reading assignment. Or they may have anecdotes they wish to share that the book has brought to mind.

Group members may prefer to put questions on cards, which you will read and discuss at appropriate times. This method ensures that you will not overlook anyone's concern.

Some groups have prepared a covenant or contract, committing themselves to complete the assigned readings prior to each session. Most participants are reluctant to break such an agreement. (See a contract you may use or paraphrase on page 33 of the Appendix. If you wish to use a contract, give a copy to each group member.)

LEAD DISCUSSION

Be sure every member has an opportunity to participate. You can do this by having each person in turn contribute to the discussion. If you find yourself leading a group in which one or two members monopolize the discussion, try limiting floor time or choosing speakers at random (by drawing names from a hat, rolling dice, or any system you choose).

Stay on the topic. Be careful not to let individual issues derail the purpose of the discussion. This is a group study and not an individual therapy session. The group cannot focus on the concerns of only one member.

DO THE ROLE-PLAYS

The role-plays may be held at the end of each session (as scheduled in the weekly timelines shown later in this book), or the group may choose to have the last session set aside to do them as a general review. The former is best for skill internalization, and that is why the role-plays were included in each session. Allow 45 minutes to one hour for this part of the session. Groups of three are the most flexible for role-playing and allow for maximum participation and use of skills. For convenience, role-plays are placed at the end of each part of the text of *Being the Parent YOU Want to Be*.

On pages 71 through 79 of the Appendix, find Role-Play Observation Sheets you can photocopy for your participants so they don't have to use the pages from their books.

We advise against personalizing the role-plays by using the names of real parents or children. This can backfire and be hurtful. The purpose of the role-plays is to give controlled practice of the skills as they are being learned. They are designed to gradually introduce the skills and allow participants to use them more effectively through practice.

STAY ON TIME

For convenience, we have assumed 2½ hours as the time frame for each session, with a break of ten to 20 minutes between the study of each skill. Adjust the times as your group sees fit. The important thing is getting consensus and sticking to it. Consistency and predictability are important for adults as well as children.

Note: Taking shorter breaks gets everyone home sooner, but taking longer breaks allows participants to discuss ideas among themselves as they are learning. Get a feel from your group members as to what will work best for them.

ORGANIZE THE SESSIONS

As you will note, *Being the Parent YOU Want to Be* is broken into six parts. Part 1 covers parenting styles. Parts 2 through 4 teach the 12 communication skills; one skill is taught in each chapter in each part. Part 5 presents the role-plays for all the skills, and Part 6 is a culminating chapter that pulls the study together.

- Session 1 in this workshop will cover Getting Acquainted and Part 1, Parenting Styles.
- Session 2 will cover Part 2, learning the four communication skills in Chapters 2 through 4, doing the practice in Chapter 5, and role-playing.
- Session 3 will cover Part 3, learning the four communication skills in Chapters 6 through 9, doing the practice in Chapter 10, and role-playing.
- Session 4 will cover Part 4, learning the four communication skills in Chapters 11 through 14, doing the practice in Chapter 15, and role-playing; it will also include Part 6, and Concluding Activities.

In each 2½-hour session, allow 20 minutes per skill or skill chapter. Each Part of the text can be covered in 1½ hours, with a ten- to 20-minute break. Then allow 20 minutes for each of the role-plays. Approximately five minutes per role-play is needed for the observer to give feedback to the parent role-player. As each role-play is completed, participants move on to the next.

END ON TIME

Adults are busy people, and they appreciate having a session not only begin on time but also end when it is scheduled to end. They may have a baby sitter at home, for example, who expects them back by a set time.

Questions that are not answered during a session can be kept for a later session. They may even serve as discussion starters for the next meeting. Often questions get answered by further reading of the book. The important thing is to start and end on time. You can always suggest that members talk to each other by phone or email during the coming week. Allow time for participants to share their phone numbers and email addresses, or photocopy a sheet with this information and give a copy to each person or family.

If you are a professional presenter, you will have a good sense of your group and can decide whether to speak with individuals with special concerns following the meeting. Avoid keeping everyone else there while you do so.

Session 1
Getting Acquainted & Part 1
"My Way, Your Way, or Our Way?"

▶ Discovering Your
Parenting Style

We have set up the following 2½-hour session as though you were holding it in the evening and beginning at 7:00 pm. Adjust the time frames to your own situation.

Materials Needed

- One or two extra texts for those who may forget theirs.
- One copy of the Group member's Information Form for each participant. (See page 34 in the Appendix.)
- Make transparencies T-1 through T-12 and T-16 through T-20. Or print transparency information on flip chart paper, duplicate it to hand out, or enter it into a Microsoft PowerPoint® presentation. (Find transparency masters in the Appendix on pages 39 through 58.)
- Overhead projector, flip chart, or Microsoft PowerPoint® presentation equipment.
- Prepared worksheets of fictional parenting styles. (See "Address the Worksheets in Part 1" below.)
- One copy of the Communication Sheet for each group member. (See the master in the Appendix on pages 35 and 36.)
- Pencil and paper for each person (optional).
- Tricky Tasks slips, one slip each for half the members of your group. (See the master in the Appendix on page 37.)

Note: Transparency T-12 is a copy of Appendix H from the book on page 335. In the first printing of the book, there was an error on the chart for the line representing Perceived Parenting Style. The points did not add up to 100 percent. We corrected this error on Transparency T-12 in this facilitator guide, and it is now improved from Appendix H in the book. If your participants are using a first printing of Being the Parent YOU Want to Be, please have them note this change on Appendix H in their books. Later printings have been corrected.

POINTS TO NOTE IN THE FIRST SESSION

Working with Participants

- On the first night, have participants share why they are taking the workshop. Whenever possible, relate their goals to something in the program. For example, if a participant says, "I want to find out how to get my children to do what I tell them without everything ending up in an argument," you might say, "You will find several useful approaches in the 'Overcoming Your Child's Objections' section. We'll cover that in the third session."

- Assure participants that answers to questions in the book are given in the text directly after the response section (they may not know this yet). If participants are uncertain of an answer, they should feel free to find it in the text. They should also bring any questions they continue to have to the following session to share and discuss with other participants, even if they are about skills in a prior section.

- Keep to the timelines. Start and end on time. Give each participant a chance to speak but not to monopolize. You can always meet with anyone who has a need for more information after the session is over.

- When seeking participants' responses and experiences, call on the participants in random order. You might even go so far as to draw numbers out of a hat to ensure that everyone has an equal opportunity to speak.

- You may have participants divide into groups of three to increase involvement. As questions arise, have the groups discuss answers among themselves and report back to the group as a whole.

Working with Session Content

- Many parents have difficulty dealing with the discovery that their perceived parenting style is not the same as the style they use. This is especially true of parents who use more "My Way" strategies than they thought they did. Stress that what is most important is that parents be congruent. They must bring their actual and perceived parenting styles together. They may do this by using more skills from the style they would like to use, or they may choose to alter their thinking and bring it in line with their practice. Each different parenting style can be effective when accompanied by warmth, understanding, nonthreatening strategies, clarity, firmness, enthusiasm, imaginativeness, task-orientation, and responsible parental behavior.

- It is more important for parents to recognize their true parenting preferences and act in accord with them than it is to choose one style over another.

Note: Range of Decision Making, on page 316 in Being the Parent YOU Want to Be, *shows which verbal skills apply to each parenting style.*

TIMELINE FOR THE FIRST SESSION

6:30 pm   Get Ready

Prepare your meeting room. Set up a refreshment area. Place an Information Form on each seat, and have participants complete it as they come in.

7:00 pm (on the dot) **Welcome!**

Icebreaker: Getting Acquainted

There are many ways to help participants get to know each other and feel comfortable working together. You may use simple introductions or come up with some special way to help members become acquainted.

7:15 pm

Overview

Give the group an overview of the four sessions so they will know what to expect. Show T-16, the skills that you will be covering in the workshop, along with a discussion of Parenting Styles.

Group Activity: Purpose — Review the Three Parenting Styles

Show the wording found on transparencies T-17, T-18, T-19, and T-20 in the Appendix to give your group a visual image to look at and refer to while you review the three styles. Use an overhead projector to show the words from the four transparencies you have copied onto flip chart paper, give participants photocopies, or show images from your Microsoft PowerPoint® presentation.

Three Parenting Styles
- "My Way"
- "Your Way"
- "Our Way"

Address the Worksheets in Part 1

Demonstrate how you or some other parent completed the worksheets in this chapter. Samples of how a fictional parent filled in each worksheet in Part 1 are found in the Appendix of *Being the Parent YOU Want to Be,* pages 330 to 335. (You also have transparency masters for these pages: T-2, T-4, T-6, T-8, T-10, and T-12.)

You might also make up responses of two imagined parents to show results that are quite different from those in the book. If you do so, choose or create sets of responses that are weighted toward opposite ends of the parenting range. Some participants might obtain similar results. Remember: There is no right style of parenting among the three styles in the book. Very likely there will be at least one participant for each style.

Discuss Group Members' Parenting Styles

Ask:

"How do you feel about what you discovered about your parenting style?"

Participants may be reluctant to speak openly. If so, be prepared to reiterate what the book says in the first and last paragraphs on page 26.

Remember: You are trying to help participants become the parents *they* want to be!

Ask:

"In which direction would you change your current style if you are not satisfied with the one you have discovered from doing the worksheets?"

8:15 pm   Break

Take a five- to ten-minute break. Tell people where the restrooms and refreshments are before breaking.

8:30 pm   Lead Discussion

Discussion Topic: The need for consistency and congruency in parent behavior.

The basic concept to discuss is that parents, teachers, and caregivers need to model the behavior they want their children to have. They should enforce rules as they were made and conveyed to their children.

Ask:

"How do you stop your child from hitting other children?"

Answer: Stop hitting your own children. The same holds true for behaviors such as smoking. Remember: "Do what you say you will do every time!"

Note: If parents don't hit children or smoke and their children have these behaviors, where are they seeing them modeled? In other words, their children are copying behaviors they have observed.

8:45 pm   Tricky Tasks

Overview

"Tricky Tasks" is the name of an activity that was created by the design team at Performance Learning Systems, publishers of this book, for use in one of their graduate courses for teachers. They have granted permission for its use in this workshop.

Tricky Tasks is a group activity that reinforces concepts of congruence and predictability. It also gives participants some interaction to help them break the ice. After completing Tricky Tasks, relate the different experiences participants had in the activity to the need for consistency and congruence in managing children. The activity is positioned at this point in the workshop specifically to reinforce the concepts presented in this session.

The Tricky Tasks activity dramatically demonstrates the challenges presented to children when learning any new task, and will, no doubt, remind your participants of how difficult learning a new task can be for children. Here, though, your participants have the advantage of being able to use their *adult* minds. Moreover, they have a wealth of experience to draw upon to make the learning much easier than a child would find it. When you finish this activity, take time to allow participants who played the child role to talk about their feelings as they tried to learn their specific tasks.

Tricky Tasks Activity

Materials Needed and Preparation: You will need a copy of the Tricky Tasks Challenge Sheet found on page 37 in the Appendix. On the sheet, you will see two lists of tasks. The two lists are identical. (One copy of the sheet will give you enough tasks for 20 pairs.) Cut the items apart so they can be passed out as slips of paper.

Directions:

1. Number off your participants — 1, 2, 1, 2 — around the room. Tell the group that those who are ones will be parents and those who are twos will be children.

2. Ask participants to form pairs that include one parent and one child — a 1 and a 2. (Ask couples in your group to find partners who are not their "significant others." Since this activity is early in the workshop, however, don't insist if people are uncomfortable with this request.)

3. Give each parent *one* of the slips of paper cut from the Tricky Tasks Challenge Sheet. (See Materials Needed above.) Tell the parents *not* to reveal to their partners the tasks that are on their slips.

4. Each parent is to train his or her child to perform the Tricky Task described on the slip of paper. The activity often begins with those who are role-playing children asking the parents what they are to do. For example, the child may ask, "Am I to stand up?" The parent is allowed to use *only one of two words* to reply: "hot" or "cold." The parent may say "hot" if the child moves toward the completion of the task or "cold" if the child moves further away from the task or makes no move at all. No other coaching is allowed.

   For example, if the parent's slip says the child is to "stand up, turn around three times, and then sit down," the parent will say "cold" if the child raises a hand. If the child leans forward as if to stand, the parent will say "hot." Should the child not stand up but lean further forward, the parent will say "cold.

5. This procedure continues until the completion time you set for the activity is up or until a set number of children successfully master their tasks.

6. You may add some pressure to the exercise by giving a prize to the "winning" child. Even more interesting can be giving a prize to the parent whose child succeeds.

7. Frequently you will see adults' egos come to the fore. Keep the challenge fun, and when a few have succeeded stop. The comments from the "unsuccessful" parents and children will often prove enlightening as all participants share their experience.

Note: Some tasks will be easy in a group on one occasion and difficult on another — just like real life!

9:15 pm   Where To From Here?

Where are we going in the next session? You may use the overhead transparency T-16 (a list of the 12 communication skills) found in the Appendix or create a handout by duplicating the list from the master. You might even choose to do both.

Ask
"What are you hoping to get from our next session?"

This Week's Homework
A word about homework: Explain the purpose of homework and the need to do it each week. It is very important for group members to share their homework results each session — the more ideas the better. The more issues the group can address, the more each participant will gain from the session.

Assignments (to be completed before Session No. 2):
• Read all of Part 2 "What Are You Thinking?" — Discovering What's On Your Child's Mind, on pages 27 through 93 in *Being the Parent YOU Want to Be.*
• Fill in all responses in the blank spaces provided. Use pencil so incorrect responses can be reviewed and erased later.
• Ask participants to come to the next session with questions or concerns they want to discuss.

Look at the section in the book called "Bridge Building," pages 91 and 92. Encourage participants to discuss the new skills with their children and find out what their children experience when the new skills are used. Encourage them to share their experiences in each session.

Again, emphasize the need to do the homework.

Diaries

As an optional assignment, ask people to start personal diaries or journals of their experiences with the skills. It would be helpful for them to bring these records to class next time and refer to them, but since diaries are personal, no one would be expected to read from them or let others see them.

9:25 pm   Communication Sheet

Overview

The Communication Sheet provides a private means by which each group member can communicate with the facilitator. Using the sheet, people can comment on the session, ask questions, and express concerns. You, in turn, will write a response on each Communication Sheet and hand it back at the beginning of the next session. These sheets help you get to know each group member better, get an indication of the tone of the group, and learn about issues you will need to address. (Research on effective group facilitation shows this type of interactive feedback adds to the quality of experience for everyone in a workshop.)

Explain the Purpose of the Communication Sheet

Give each participant his or her own Communication Sheet. Explain to group members the purpose and manner of completing the Communication Sheet. There is an explanation on each sheet as well.

Complete Communication Sheets

Allow several minutes for participants to write. Then collect the sheets or indicate a place in the room where participants can leave them at the end of the session.

9:30 pm   Dismiss on Time!

Session 2
Part 2
"What Are You Thinking?"

····▶ Discovering
What's On Your
Child's Mind

Materials Needed

- One or two extra texts for those who may have forgotten theirs.
- Make transparencies T-21, T-22, T-23, and T-24. Or print transparency information on flip chart paper, put it into a Microsoft PowerPoint® presentation, or duplicate the masters as handouts. (You will find masters in the Appendix on page 59 through 62.)
- Reproduce T-16 (the 12 communication skills) if you haven't already.
- Overhead projector, flip chart, or Microsoft PowerPoint® presentation equipment.
- Communication Sheets to be returned with your written replies.
- Your own examples for each skill.
- Make Role-Play Observation Sheets from masters T-33a, T-33b, and T-33c if you would prefer people not write in their books. (Find the masters on pages 71 through 73 in the Appendix.) You will need one of each for every person if you intend each person to play each role during the session — as we suggest. (*Note: These Observation Sheets are also in the text on pages 279 to 281.*)
- Pencil and paper for each person (optional).

POINTS TO NOTE IN THE SECOND SESSION
Working with Session Content

- Keep in mind that the key difference between the Tell-Me-What's-On-Your-Mind Question (TWM) and the Give-Me-Specific-Information Question (GSI) is control. GSI Questions lead directly to the parent's goal. TWM Questions give children more opportunity to explain their agendas. A TWM series of questions usually takes longer too. Such a series has the advantage of helping children explore alternatives and exercise their reasoning skills. It may also prove more productive, because these questions allow children latitude of thought, and greater use of imagination, discrimination skills, and judgment.

- GSI strategies take less time and may lead more directly to a conclusion. The parent must avoid an "Aha, I've got you!" attitude.

- Sometimes questions make statements. An example: "Haven't you done your homework yet?" The child usually hears— and often the parent means to imply — "You certainly should have by now!" The question "Have you finished your homework yet?" has a better chance of reducing the child's hostility. Positive Phrasing has the effect of reducing children's resistance to parents' authority. Positive Phrasing is less confrontational and raises fewer defenses. (*Note: Positive Phrasing means refraining from stating something in the negative. You want to avoid implying "no" by using words like "don't" and "haven't." It also means to say what you do want rather than what you don't want. The Look-On-The-Bright-Side Statement is another label for Positive Phrasing.*)

- If parents use questions that make statements, they should be very careful to be aware of their body language and intonation. They need to use neutral and positive language.

- Show how body language can affect communication. Ask for a parent volunteer to sit while you stand over him or her with your arms crossed, your lips pursed, and a stern expression on your face. Say, "I'm really happy you are here." Ask how the volunteer feels, and you will discover that the parent will nearly always express discomfort. The incongruity is readily seen. Children feel the same way. Remind participants that our body language must match our words. Doing a similar demonstration, this time with your arms loose or reaching to shake the volunteer's hand, wearing a smile, and making eye contact, can reinforce this. Warmly say, "I'm really happy you are here."

- What happens when parents confirm facts not on their children's agendas? Or what if the parent confirms a fact and the child is expressing an attitude or feeling? Point out that the parent still receives valuable information from the child's response. The parent still learns what is on the child's mind. Consider:

Child: I didn't do the dishes.
Parent: You forgot.
Child: I was having too much fun, and I didn't want to come in.

While intending to confirm a fact with a What-You-Meant Statement (WYM), the parent discovered the child's attitude. The WYM Statement produced information.

- Whenever children are motivated from within rather than from without (by the parent), they have a greater stake in any change that takes place. The same is true when *they* own their behavior and that ownership is not forced upon them. That's why Think-It-Over Statements (TIO) are so useful. When given in a nonjudgmental tone that implies a true desire to understand rather than criticize, the TIO Statement simply points out incongruities for children to see for themselves.

- To demonstrate to those who doubt that children who are motivated from within have a greater stake in any change that takes place, try a few GSI Questions. In doing so you may elicit the defensive reaction the TIO Statement is intended to avoid. Be sure to debrief any parents you try this with to clarify that you were simply trying to demonstrate the problem; make it clear that you were not challenging them. If in doubt, ask for a volunteer and demonstrate how the challenge really looks.

- Go over again the need to keep body language, words, and intonation congruent. With the TIO Statement, it is particularly important to remain matter-of-fact, even lighthearted at times. Sarcasm must be avoided at all costs, as must any implication that the child is stupid or childish. Respect a child's right to have his or her feelings and ideas. Giving more information is more likely to lead children to reexamine their thinking than is an outright challenge or showing you are "smarter" than they.

- Parents' TIO Statements must always be delivered in a nonjudgmental fashion.

- Point out that parents must avoid an "Aha, I've got you!" reaction when using the TIO Statement. When this parental reaction is conveyed to children, they may feel the parent is gloating. They may feel the parent is saying, "I'm smarter than you." Rather, listen to all that the child has to say, avoiding any hint of parental "victory."

- Body language when using the TIO Statement is very important. You may want to use one or two volunteers to demonstrate the impact of body language and voice intonation on what the parent says to the child.

Role-Plays

- You may choose to do some of the role-plays in any or all of the appropriate sessions. Point out to participants that role-plays were designed to give them the opportunity to select and verbalize the various skills in the manner and for the purpose intended.

- It is important that every participant in a role-play has the opportunity to play the roles of parent, child, and observer at least once. That is why triads are used. When only a pair is possible, the child role-player can also serve as observer. Or you may choose to participate in the group. It is preferable that participants work on their own, however, because the presence of the facilitator may inhibit participants from taking risks with each other. If one person is left over after triads are formed, have that participant join one of the triads.

- Allow enough time for participants to read the instructions and background information for each role-play. About 15 to 20 minutes to perform each role-play is usually sufficient, including five minutes for the observer to give feedback.

- Participants are to read only the information that relates to the role they are playing.

- Emphasize the need for parent role-players to name the skill they are going to use before they use it. While this may seem unnatural (it is), doing so alerts the observers to what they are to listen for and will help in debriefing parent role-players later. (Example: "Mary, when John told you how he felt, you said you were going to use a WYM Statement. You actually used a TIO Statement. Did you notice John's reaction?") Naming a skill before delivering it also helps participants internalize the verbal pattern of the skill and better understand when to use it.
- Parent role-players should focus primarily on the skills of the current section, though using other skills will sometimes be unavoidable.
- Encourage child role-players to be difficult and stubborn enough to allow many opportunities for parent role-players to use the skills focused on in this session.
- The facilitator should circulate among the groups, never staying longer than a few minutes near one group. This will prevent participants from becoming self-conscious and inhibited.
- The observers should give the Role-Play Observation Sheets to the parent role-players immediately after debriefing at the end of each role-play.
- Take time at the end of the role-plays to discuss successes and concerns.

TIMELINE FOR THE SECOND SESSION

6:30 pm   Setup

Set up the tables, chairs, and refreshments. Have the Communication Sheets available to hand back as group members arrive.

7:00 pm   Welcome Everyone Back

Ask:
"Would any of you be willing to share your experiences with the skills during the past week?"

Answer questions regarding homework and fill-in-the-blank responses.

Return the Communication Sheets with your written responses to each person.

7:15 pm   Review the Four Skills in Part 2

Using overhead transparencies T-21 through T-24, a flip chart copy, duplicated pages for each participant, or a Microsoft PowerPoint® presentation, review each of the four skills in Part 2 and their uses.

Give additional examples of how group members might use the skills.

7:45 pm   Group Work

Place group members into small groups of two or three people. Each group's task is to come up with new examples of each of the four skills and present their examples to the other participants.

Groups Share Examples

Focusing on one skill at a time, ask each group to share its best example of each skill. If a skill is used incorrectly in the example, point out which skill *is* being used. (It is more than likely that the example will demonstrate another skill, possibly even one not learned yet.) Then ask for an example of a correct use of the skill, or supply an example of your own. Be prepared for such eventualities with examples of each skill.

8:15 pm   Break

8:30 pm   Role-Plays

You will find instructions for the role-plays in Part 5 of *Being the Parent YOU Want to Be: 12 Communication Skills for Effective Parenting.* Look for general instructions on pages 271 to 272.

Role-plays for this session, "Discovering What's On Your Child's Mind," are in Chapter 16 on pages 273 through 278.

Use the Role-Play Observation Sheets on pages 279 through 281 of the text, or make copies from the masters available in the Appendix (T-33a, T-33b, T33c). You may use an overhead transparency, a flip chart page, or a Microsoft PowerPoint® presentation to demonstrate how to fill in a sample sheet.

Allow 45 minutes to one hour for the role-plays — 15 to 20 minutes for each one. Approximately five minutes of the 15 or 20 minutes is needed for the observer to give feedback to the parent role-player. As each role-play is completed, participants move on to the next.

Remember: We advise against personalizing the role-plays by using the names of real parents or children.

9:15 pm   Where To From Here?

To introduce the next session, use the overhead transparency T-16 (the 12 communication skills) in the Appendix (page 54) or a handout you have duplicated from the master. You might even choose to do both. Next session you will be focusing on the skills in Part 3: "Overcoming Your Child's Objections."

Ask:
"What are you hoping to get from the next session?"

This Week's Homework

Remind participants of the purpose of homework and the need to do it each week. It is very important for participants to share their homework results each session — the more ideas the better. The more issues the group can address, the more each participant will gain from the session.

Assign Homework:

Read all of Part 3: "I Don't Want To!" — Overcoming Your Child's Objections on pages 95 through 183.

Remember to fill in all responses in the blank spaces provided. Use a pencil so incorrect responses can be reviewed and erased later.

Diaries

Participants who did so last week should continue to keep a personal diary of experiences they have using the skills. Those who did not keep a diary last week may want to start one. Ask those who did keep a diary to talk about their experience.

Again, encourage participants to discuss the new skills with their children and find out what their children experience when the new skills are used. Encourage them also to share this feedback in each session.

Remind participants to come with questions or concerns they want to discuss in the next session.

9:25 pm   **Communication Sheets**

Allow participants a few minutes to complete their Communication Sheets and turn them in.

9:30 pm   **Dismiss on Time!**

Session 3
Part 3
"I Don't Want To!"

:
:
:
. . . . . ▶ Overcoming Your
Child's Objections

Materials Needed
- One or two extra texts for those who may forget theirs.
- Make transparencies T-25 through T-28 or print transparency information on flip chart paper, duplicate it to hand out, or put it into a Microsoft PowerPoint® presentation. (You will find the masters in the Appendix on pages 63 through 66.)
- Reproduce T-16 (the 12 communication skills) if you haven't already.
- Reproduce Role-Play Observation Sheets T-34a, T-34b, and T-34c — one of each for each person. (Find the masters on pages 74 through 76 in the Appendix.)
- Overhead projector, flip chart, or Microsoft PowerPoint® presentation equipment.
- Communication Sheets to be returned with your replies written in.
- Your own examples for each skill.
- Pencil and paper for each person (optional).

POINTS TO NOTE IN THE THIRD SESSION
Working with Session Content
- Emphasize that the importance of this session is to help participants become more positive. Positive is always better!
- Positive phrasing (the Look-On-The-Bright-Side Statement) should be a part of every skill. The Walk-In-Their-Shoes Statement (WITS) is particularly useful for dealing with emotional resistance, the Support-Their-Thinking Statement (STT) for intellectual resistance, and the Catch-Them-Doing-It-Right Statement (CTDR) for healing hurt pride.
- Parents will often have difficulty with the notion that even negative behavior can have positive elements. For example, a child caught plagiarizing materials from the Internet clearly wants to pass. He or she may have shown ability to research the site where the contents for a paper could be found. The child certainly had to formulate a plan. While in no way do parents want to condone dishonesty, they will make more progress with their children if they at least recognize the positive

15

attributes displayed. The real goal is to redirect these positives in more constructive directions. Doing so requires a positive mental set. Empathy (not sympathy) and acceptance of the child do not need to mean agreement; they just work better. And since a child caught plagiarizing a paper is likely to receive a failing grade on the paper (if not the course), nothing more in that regard need be said. Rather, more will be gained by helping the child find better ways to succeed and more constructive ways to use the skills the child has demonstrated. Still, recognizing the positive aspects of negative behavior goes against our grain in many cases. Stress the fact that positive works!

- The Support-Their-Thinking Statement (STT) can be the most challenging skill of this section. It is important to accept children's viewpoints and acknowledge that they *believe* they have good reasons to do what they do. Such acknowledgment does not have to imply that the parent agrees. To change a child's thinking, parents must redirect their attention to the *child's* reasons and start from there. Only then is the child's point of view likely to change. Used properly, STT Statements and TIO Statements will go a long way in this direction.

- Help parents understand that the reason they like to do the things they do is that they are usually reasonably good at them. The reason they avoid other activities is that they are usually not so good at them. We like to experience success! Children are no different. Their self-esteem is enhanced when they succeed or get positive feedback on their efforts. When children meet with failure, seeing the glass half full rather than half empty will encourage them to keep trying. Knowing they were making progress has kept many future champions going until they succeeded.

- By pointing out what is wrong rather than what is right, parents leave out an important part — perhaps the most important part — of learning. Look-On-The-Bright-Side Statements (LOBS) support learning by pointing out what to do rather than what not to do. Catching a ball properly, for example, is clearly more important than avoiding dropping it. (How many times do adults say to kids: "Don't drop the ball.") Some players have been seen to drop a ball only to catch it again before it hit the ground. Catching, not dropping the ball won the game! (Using positive phrasing, the adults should say: "Catch the ball.")

- One parent has a habit of pointing out how her children are progressing. She never points out what other kids are doing. Rather, she tells her children how much better *they* are doing something now than they did earlier. She stresses, for example, how many more correct answers they got on their most recent test rather than how many mistakes they made. You can be sure her kids keep trying to better their own scores. They are not threatened with mother comparing them to another student. Their mother shows them that what *they* are doing is important to her, not what other kids are doing. Every day she says, "I have confidence in your ability to keep learning."

- Briefly point out the need to phrase statements positively *all* the time. "Don't put the milk in first" falls far short of "Put the flour in before you add the milk."

- As with the questioning skills, these statement skills get their impact from both voice intonation and from the words themselves. Body language is also important. Remind participants of the need for congruence and being positive.

- Ask participants to describe themselves in terms of the characteristics they're most proud of — honorable, kind, cheerful, encouraging, hard-working, dependable, gentle, organized, studious, etc. When these characteristics are recognized, parents are confirmed; they feel valued when approved of for demonstrating these characteristics. Point out to participants that they did not all value the same characteristics. Realizing that different people value different forms of approval helps parents understand how a particular form of approval works at some times and not at others and with one child and not another. For approval to be effective, it must be legitimate, specific, and credible *in the mind of the one approved.* Therefore, parents must connect approval to children's values. Praising a child for being tidy will do little good when the child doesn't care about tidiness but does care about fixing things well.

- If you want children to repeat behavior that is not connected to characteristics they value, tell them how you were affected by what they did; for example, "I really appreciated your taking out the garbage. No one likes that job. Now I have time for us to . . ." The reward is the time you can spend together or simply your sincere appreciation. This works especially well when you show your willingness to help in return.

- While approval is encouraging, too much of it can have just the opposite effect. I learned this the hard way. I once praised a child for a very excellent drawing she had made. I put it on the bulletin board and told many others about it. She immediately quit drawing in my class. I discovered that my excesses had made her feel that she might not be able to top her achievement, and she decided to quit while she was ahead. The following year I saw a piece of work she had done and told her I liked the way she made her trees. She began to show me her work again. We can overdo approval. Approval must be realistic, specific, encouraging, and legitimate.

- It is better, for example, to say to a child, "I appreciate you helping with the dishes" than to say "What a good boy for doing the dishes." Goodness and doing dishes are not connected; helpfulness and tidiness certainly are!

- Approving only those behaviors that merit approval legitimizes them. Approving insignificant achievements diminishes not only real achievements but the child as well. Think about how you would feel if someone said to you, "I like the way you hold your fork. You certainly have good table manners." If you were just learning how to use a fork, this might be legitimate approval — certainly not if you were a typical adult.

- Sometimes hurt pride or hurt feelings may be masked as intellectualization. You can usually determine if this is so by listening to a child's tone of voice or looking at his or her body language. Sometimes the situation will reveal which is in play. Especially when children show an argumentative spirit, they are likely to be masking issues of pride. Use Support-Their-Thinking Statements whenever you suspect pride is at issue. Walk-In-Their-Shoes and Catch-Them-Doing-It-Right Statements can come into play later.

- Emphasize the need for parents to tune in not only to *what* children are saying but also *how* they are saying it. Listen to the words, but also hear the intonation and watch the body language. These provide important clues to a child's agenda and resistances.

Role-Plays

- You may choose to do some of the role-plays in any or all of the appropriate sessions. Point out to participants that role-plays were designed to give them the opportunity to select and verbalize the various skills in the manner and for the purpose intended.
- It is important that every participant in a role-play has the opportunity to play the roles of parent, child, and observer at least once. That is why triads are used. When only a pair is possible, the child role-player can also serve as observer. Or you may choose to participate in the group. It is preferable that participants work on their own, however, because the presence of the facilitator may inhibit participants from taking risks with each other. If one person is left over after triads are formed, have that participant join one of the triads.
- Allow enough time for participants to read the instructions and background information for each role-play. About 15 to 20 minutes to perform each role-play is usually sufficient, including five minutes for the observer to give feedback.
- Participants are to read only the information that relates to the role they are playing.
- Emphasize the need for parent role-players to name the skill they are going to use before they use it. While this may seem unnatural (it is), doing so alerts the observers to what they are to listen for and will help in debriefing parent role-players later. (Example: "Michael, when Megan told you how she felt, you said you were going to use a WITS Statement. You actually used a STT Statement. Did you notice Megan's reaction?") Naming a skill before delivering it also helps participants internalize the verbal pattern of the skill and better understand when to use it.
- Parent role-players should focus primarily on the skills of the current section, though using other skills will sometimes be unavoidable.
- Encourage child role-players to be difficult and stubborn enough to allow many opportunities for parent role-players to use the skills focused on in this session.
- The facilitator should circulate among the groups, never staying longer than a few minutes near one group. This will prevent participants from becoming self-conscious and inhibited.
- The observers should give the Role-Play Observation Sheets to the parent role-players immediately after debriefing at the end of each role-play.
- Take time at the end of the role-plays to discuss successes and concerns.

TIMELINE FOR THE THIRD SESSION

6:30 pm   Setup

Set up chairs, tables, and refreshments. Be ready to give back Communication Sheets, if that is your routine.

7:00 pm   Welcome Everyone Back

Ask:
"Do we have volunteers who will relate their experiences with the skills since we last met?"

Answer questions about homework and fill-in-the-blank responses.

7:15 pm   Review the Four Skills in Part 3

Using transparencies T-25 through T-28, a flip chart, duplicated pages, or a Microsoft PowerPoint® presentation, go over the steps in each of the skills.

7:45 pm   Group Work

Arrange group members in small groups of two or three. If you have members of the same family in your session, ask them to join separate groups. Have groups come up with examples of each of the four skills.

Groups Share Examples

Focusing on one skill at a time, ask each group to share its best example of each skill. If a skill is used incorrectly in the example, point out which skill *is* being used. (It is more than likely that the example will demonstrate another skill, even one not learned yet.) Then ask for an example of a correct use of the skill, or supply an example of your own. Be prepared for such eventualities with examples of each skill.

8:15 pm   Break

8:30 pm   Role-Plays

You will find instructions for the role-plays in Part 5 of *Being the Parent YOU Want to Be: 12 Communication Skills for Effective Parenting*. Look for general instructions on pages 271 and 272.

Role-plays for this session, "Overcoming Your Child's Objections," are in Chapter 17 on pages 283 through 289.

The Role-Play Observation Sheets for the role-plays are on pages 290 through 292 of the text. You may want to make an overhead transparency, a flip chart page, or a Microsoft PowerPoint® presentation of one of these sheets to show how to fill it in (unless participants recall how to do so from the previous session). If you don't want people to write in their books, pass out duplicates of T-34a, T-34b, and T-34c to each person. These are found on pages 74 through 76 in the Appendix.

9:15 pm   Where To From Here?

To introduce the next session, use overhead transparency T-16 (the 12 communication skills) found in the Appendix (page 54) or a handout you have duplicated from the master. (You might even choose to do both.) You are going to focus on Part 4: "Solving Problems and Making Decisions With Your Child."

Ask:
"What are you hoping to get from the last session?"

This Week's Homework
Remind participants of the purpose of homework and the need to do it each week. It is very important for participants to share their homework results each session. The more ideas the better. The more issues the group can address, the more each participant will gain from the session.

Assign Homework
Read all of Part 4: "What WILL We Do?" — Solving Problems and Making Decisions With Your Child, pages 185 through 265, and all of Part 6: "Put It All Together," pages 305 through 326.

Remember to fill in all responses in the blank spaces provided. Use a pencil so incorrect responses can be reviewed and erased later. In Part 6, fill in the worksheet.

Diaries
Participants who have been doing so should continue to keep a personal diary of experiences they have using the skills. Those who have not been keeping a diary may want to start one. You could ask those who did keep a diary to talk about their experience.

Again, encourage participants to discuss the new skills with their children and find out what their children experience when new skills are tried out. Encourage them also to share this feedback in each session.

Remind participants to come with questions or concerns they want to discuss in the next session.

9:25 pm   Communication Sheets

Have participants complete their Communication Sheets and turn them in before they leave.

9:30 pm   Dismiss on Time!

Session 4
Part 4 "What WILL We Do?" &
Part 6 "Put It All Together"

▶ Solving Problems and
Making Decisions
With Your Child
& Concluding
Activities

Materials Needed

- One or two extra texts in case someone forgets theirs.
- Make transparencies T-29, T-30, T-31, and T-32. Or print transparency information on flip chart paper, duplicate it to hand out, or put it into a Microsoft PowerPoint® presentation. (You will find transparency masters in the Appendix on pages 67 through 70.)
- Overhead projector, flip chart, or Microsoft PowerPoint® presentation equipment.
- Reproduce T-16 (the 12 communication skills) if you haven't already.
- Reproduce T-13, T-14, and T-15. (See pages 51 through 53 in the Appendix.)
- Reproduce Role-Play Observation Sheets T-35a, T-35b, and T-35c — one of each for each person. (They are on pages 77 through 79 in the Appendix.)
- Communication Sheets to be returned with your written replies.
- Your own examples for each skill.
- Evaluation Sheets, one per person. (See page 38 in the Appendix for the master.)
- Pencil and paper for each person (optional).

POINTS TO NOTE IN THE FOURTH SESSION

Working with Session Content

- Point out that a Hobson's Choice, used with a Solve-The-Problem Question (STP), while very much a "My Way" strategy, allows the child to feel he or she has a choice. Having any choice often gives the child a feeling that he or she still has some control. It is a better option than giving no choice at all in that it gets more

21

cooperation and meets with less resistance and resentment. (See page 208 in the text for the definition of Hobson's Choice.)

- Clarify the control element in the choice of how to phrase a This-Is-The-Deal Statement (TTD) — either "If you do this, I will do that" or "If I do this, you will do that." The real power is always in the hands of the parent, regardless of which phrasing is used, because the parent decides who must take the initiative in the bargain. Nevertheless, children feel *they* have control when the parent takes the initiative ("If I do this, you will do that"). In either case, the purpose of the TTD Statement is to get an agreement between the parent and the child.

- When using the TTD, the parent should take the initiative whenever he or she feels the child will commit. If there is a doubt, require the child to perform first, then the parent can reciprocate. It is important, too, that the child do what is required.

- Criticism, however well-intentioned, can hurt. When people are criticized, they become defensive. The Out-Of-Bounds Statement (OB) can reduce this defensiveness. Moreover, it can prevent children from banding together in resistance to the parent. Here is a demonstration, somewhat altered from one used in *Being the Parent YOU Want to Be:*

    Before the session begins, ask for the help of a participant with whom you feel comfortable working. Agree beforehand that just before you introduce the Out-Of-Bound Statement, you will give your volunteer a prearranged signal to drop his or her pencil. When the pencil drops, attack your participant verbally by saying something like "Can't you hold on to that? What's the matter, butterfingers?" Wait a few moments, and then ask participants for their reactions to your remarks — if they haven't commented already.

    What you want to show is that such criticisms make not only the one attacked defensive but also those around that person. Everyone feels vulnerable and open to attack. Such attacks lead others to side with the "victim" against the "attacker." Letting participants experience this reaction will make them more aware of why children band together against the parent when a sibling or friend is put down in front of them.

    Having seen the effect of such critical comments, participants will be more receptive to the use of the Out-Of-Bounds Statement, which prevents children from forming alliances against what they perceive as a bullying parent.

- The Out-Of-Bounds Statement is effective because it shows disapproval only of the child's actions, not the child. It is impersonal in this sense. It tells the child that the parent doesn't like what the child did, but that the parent still likes the child. This is "acceptance without agreement."

- Keep in mind: Children can change their behavior; they cannot change who they are.

- Often when parents want to use a Do-It-This-Way (DITW) Statement, they first use an Out-Of-Bounds Statement. For example:

Parent (to children throwing a ball in the living room): "That ball is going to break something. *Take it outside and play catch there.*"

   An Out-Of-Bounds Statement precedes the Do-It-This-Way Statement in italics. While this approach is not wrong, the parent could have focused on the behavior rather than the children themselves and said, "Take the ball outside and play catch there." Most children would see the logic behind this Do-It-This-Way Statement that implies the ball could damage things if thrown in the house.

- With an older child, often all a parent needs to do is tell the child what is to be done. For younger children, the reason for a directive is often necessary. For example, an older child understands why running in the house may not be a good idea, while a younger child may need to learn that running in the house could lead to a bad fall or injury. When in doubt, give the reason for any Do-It-This-Way Statement rather than imply it.

Role-Plays
- You may choose to do role-plays in this session. Point out to participants that role-plays were designed to give them the opportunity to select and verbalize the various skills in the manner and for the purpose intended.
- It is important that every participant in a role-play has the opportunity to play the roles of parent, child, and observer at least once. That is why triads are used. When only a pair is possible, the child role-player can also serve as observer. Or you may choose to participate in the group. It is preferable that participants work on their own, however, because the presence of the facilitator may inhibit participants from taking risks with each other. If one person is left over after triads are formed, have that participant join one of the triads.
- Allow enough time for participants to read the instructions and background information for each role-play. About 15 to 20 minutes to perform each role-play is usually sufficient, including five minutes for the observer to give feedback.
- Participants are to read only the information that relates to the role they are playing.
- Emphasize the need for parent role-players to name the skill they are going to use before they use it. While this may seem unnatural (it is), doing so alerts the observers to what they are to listen for and will help in debriefing parent role-players later. (Example: "Sarah, when Michael stated his problem, you said you were going to ask an STP Question. You actually used a TTD Statement. Did you notice Michael's reaction?") Naming a skill before delivering it also helps participants internalize the verbal pattern of the skill and better understand when to use it.

- Parent role-players should focus primarily on the skills of the current section, though using other skills will sometimes be unavoidable.
- Encourage child role-players to be difficult and stubborn enough to allow many opportunities for parent role-players to use the skills focused on in this session.
- The facilitator should circulate among the groups, never staying longer than a few minutes near one group. This will prevent participants from becoming self-conscious and inhibited.
- The observers should give the Role-Play Observation Sheets to the parent role-players immediately after debriefing at the end of each role-play.
- Take time at the end of the role-plays to discuss successes and concerns.

TIMELINE FOR THE FOURTH SESSION

6:30 pm   Setup

Set up chairs, tables, and refreshments. Be ready to return Communication Sheets if that is your routine.

7:00 pm   Welcome Everyone Back

Ask:
"Do we have volunteers who will relate their experiences with the skills during the past week?"

Answer questions about homework and fill-in-the-blank responses.

7:15 pm   Review the Four Skills in Part 4

Using transparencies T-29 through T-32, a flip chart, duplicated pages, or a Microsoft PowerPoint® presentation, go over the steps in each of the skills.

7:45 pm   Group Work

Arrange group members in small groups of two or three. If you have members of the same family in your session, ask them to please join separate groups. Have groups come up with examples of each of the four skills.

Groups Share Examples

Focusing on one skill at a time, ask each group to share its best example of each skill. If a skill is used incorrectly in the example, point out which skill *is* being used. (It is more than likely that the example will demonstrate another skill.) Then ask for an example of a correct use of the skill, or supply an example of your own. Be prepared for such eventualities with examples of each skill.

8:15 pm   Break

8:30 pm   Role-Plays

You will find the instructions for the role-plays in Part 5 of *Being the Parent YOU Want to Be: 12 Communication Skills for Effective Parenting*. Look for general instructions on pages 271 and 272.

Role-plays for this session, "Solving Problems and Making Decisions With Your Child," are in Chapter 18 on pages 293 through 299.

The Role-Play Observation Sheets are on pages 300 through 302 in the text. Or, if you don't want people to write in their books, make copies of those pages using T-35a, T-35b, and T-35c from the masters in the Appendix on pages 77 through 79. You may want to make an overhead transparency, a flip chart page, or a Microsoft PowerPoint® presentation of one of these sheets to show how to fill it in (unless your participants recall how it was done in the last two sessions).

9:15 pm   Pull It All Together

Have participants discuss their experience with the 12 verbal skills.

Ask:
"Which skills did you find difficult to use?"

"Which were easy?"

"Which are still giving you trouble?"

Confirm Parenting Styles
Have participants consider their parenting styles again.

Ask:
"Has your parenting style changed?"

"Are you more confirmed in your style?"

If you have time, use Worksheet 6 on T-13 (and the sample on T-14).

Using T-15, go over "Range of Decision Making." It is found on page 316 in the text.

AND/OR

Review the 12 Verbal Skills

Review the skills and go over how to use them. To do this, name the skill and ask what steps are used to implement it. Have participants give examples of phrases they would use to implement the skill. (T-15, "Range of Decision Making," would be helpful. It is found on page 316 in the text.)

For example, ask:

"What are the two steps of the Walk-In-Their-Shoes Statement?"

"Using those two steps, give a Walk-In-Their-Shoes Statement."

"When would you use a Do-It-This-Way Statement?"

"Give an example of a skill from this workshop you now use with your children, including the results."

9:25 pm   Communication Sheet and Evaluation

Communication Sheets

Ask participants to write their last comments on the Communication Sheets. Either collect the Communication Sheets or allow participants to keep them. If you want to respond to their final comments, collect the sheets and mail them back to participants at a later date. Tell them you will do so. (If you mail them, use the mailing as an opportunity to let them know about future workshops you will be providing. Also encourage them to keep using the skills.)

Evaluation Sheets

Distribute and then collect the Evaluation Sheets (master found on page 38) as soon as participants complete them. These sheets are for your information. Or, if you facilitated this workshop for a particular school or organization, give the Evaluation Sheets (or copies of them) to the organization so that they can be used to evaluate the workshop's effectiveness.

Thank You

Be sure to thank participants for being a part of the workshop experience and for their diligent work. Tell them about future workshops so that they can pass the word to friends and colleagues.

9:30 pm   Dismiss on Time!

APPENDIX OF
REPRODUCIBLE PAGES

TABLE OF CONTENTS

DEAR PARENT/CAREGIVER:

Our group is about to begin an exciting new program designed to help you communicate better with your children.

The program is based on the book *Being the Parent YOU Want to Be: 12 Communication Skills for Effective Parenting.* This book discusses three parenting styles and 12 communication skills. It is easy to read and has practice opportunities built in as you read along.

The program will meet for four sessions.
Please note the location, dates, and times:

Location: _____

Session 1:_____

Session 2:_____

Session 3:_____

Session 4_____

The text for the course is available: _____

_____

You must complete reading assignments before the first session meets. Attached you will find these assignments.

Please bring your book to the first session.

If you have questions, please feel free to call me at _____.

Sincerely,

Group Facilitator

Reading Assignments

GENERAL DIRECTIONS:

Congratulations on your enrollment in our parenting skills workshop! You will be learning 12 valuable communication skills that will aid you not only in parenting but in communicating with people throughout your life.

The text for the workshop will be the book *Being the Parent YOU Want to Be: 12 Communication Skills for Effective Parenting.* The facilitator of your group will provide the book for you or tell you how you can purchase it on your own.

To prepare for discussion of the communication skills in *Being the Parent YOU Want to Be: 12 Communication Skills for Effective Parenting,* you will need to read sections of the book prior to each workshop session.

It is important that you complete the appropriate readings *before* each session so that you will be ready to discuss them during the session. It is recommended that you make a list of questions that come to mind as you read. Bring these questions to your next session. They will add to the discussion, and you will be able to hear how others in the group have dealt with those and similar questions of their own. Your active participation will enrich the experience of everyone in the group.

Please complete any exercises and fill in any blanks, as appropriate, with pencil. Reviewing each section later, you will then be able to erase incorrect or incomplete responses and replace them with accurate ones.

Some parents, teachers, and caregivers find that it is helpful to keep a diary of their experiences with the skills as the program moves along.

MATERIALS NEEDED:

You will need a copy of *Being the Parent YOU Want to Be.* **Take the book with you to each session. Put your name in your copy.**

It will also be helpful for you to bring a pencil or a pen and a pad of paper to each workshop session.

Depending on the plans of your facilitator, you might also be asked to bring snacks to share with the group.

BEFORE SESSION 1: READ PAGES IX THROUGH 26 IN
BEING THE PARENT YOU WANT TO BE.

Date of Session 1: _____

Survey the Table of Contents. Read the Foreword, Acknowledgments, and Introduction. From them you will get an overview of the program. Read about the three parenting styles: My Way, Your Way, and Our Way. Complete the activities, worksheets, and exercises. Enjoy the illustrations as well. They, too, will aid your understanding of the materials. Write down questions you have, and take them with you to the first session. Also be sure to take a copy of the book to each session.

Consider keeping a personal diary of your experiences with the skills. This will help you remember them. Share your experiences with others in the group during Session 1.

BEFORE SESSION 2: READ PAGES 27 THROUGH 93

Date of Session 2: _____

As you complete the exercises and fill in the blanks in this section of the book, you will be learning the skills that will help you discover what is on your child's mind.

You might also want to keep a personal diary of your experiences with the skills — those that are successful and those that are not so successful. You will learn from both kinds of experiences, and it is expected that you won't use the skills perfectly the first time. Nor will your children necessarily respond as you might wish. Keeping the diary will enable you to see how you grow in your mastery of the skills and may jog your memory during discussions in the various sessions.

For those who have been keeping a personal diary, consider how it has helped. Would you recommend that other parents keep such a diary? Why or why not? Share your experiences with others in the group during Session 2.

We also encourage you to discuss with your child his or her experience of your use of the new skills. Do not be surprised if at first your child seems a little more difficult than usual. You are changing your child's environment, and when you do that the child will almost always test the change to see if it is permanent or not.

BEFORE SESSION 3: READ PAGES 95 THROUGH 183.

Date of Session 3: _____

In these chapters you will learn four skills that will help you overcome your child's resistance to your authority. Like us, children do not change easily. They change gradually in response to changes in their environment. The communication skills in Chapters 6 to 10 of *Being the Parent YOU Want to Be* help you gain your child's cooperation. They will help you get your child to do what is wanted and needed.

Have you been keeping a personal diary? Has it helped? Would you recommend that other parents keep such a diary? Why or why not? Share your experiences with others in the group during Session 3.

BEFORE SESSION 4: READ PAGES 185 THROUGH 265.
ALSO READ PAGES 305 TO 326.

Date of Session 4: _____

The last four skills will help you help your children to solve problems and make responsible decisions. The skills in this section will also help you set limits for your children and minimize their objections while doing so. Yes, there will still be conflicts between you and your child from time to time. With these skills and the others you have already covered, there will be fewer of them and they will usually be less intense.

Read the last chapter and fill out Worksheet 6 on page 312.

Note: We skip Part 5 because it is about the role-plays, which are done during workshop sessions.

How is your diary coming along? By now you probably have many interesting entries. Remember to take the time to write in it. This journal will be a source of encouragement as you continue to master the skills of *Being the Parent YOU Want to Be.*

Participation Contract

for a workshop in which I will be learning the communication skills in

Being the Parent YOU Want to Be:
12 Communication Skills for Effective Parenting
by Gary Screaton Page

I, _____, agree to come prepared for each session of the workshop. I commit myself to doing the assigned readings before each session, completing all projects and activities, bringing my book to class, and sharing my experiences with the other members of the group.

Signature _____ Date_____

Performance Learning Systems grants facilitator of this program the right to photocopy this page for use in group sessions.

Group Member's Information Form

Please help us by sharing the following information with your facilitator. Feel free to omit any information you do not wish to share. Information will be kept confidential.

Name   _____

Address   _____

             _____

Daytime Phone _____ Evening Phone _____

Email _____ Fax _____

No. of children presently in your home or in your care _____

No. of female children _____ Ages _____

No. of male children _____ Ages _____

Type of residence ☐ house ☐ apartment ☐ Other (specify) _____
(This information is useful because the type of living situation sometimes affects the rules that must be made for children.)

What do you hope to gain from participation in this group?

What three questions about communicating with children would you most like to have answered? (Use the reverse side if needed.)

Communication Sheet

This form offers you and the facilitator a place to exchange ideas privately. Indicate your evaluation of each session, and make any comments you would like about the experiences you are having in the group. Your responses will be kept confidential.

- What did you find most helpful?
- Least helpful?
- What would you like to have discussed during the next session?
- Do you have questions?

These and other comments should be entered into the Participant Response space. The facilitator will respond in his or her space between sessions. If you have an urgent concern, please make this known and the facilitator will contact you. Let him or her know the best time you can be reached. Thank you.

SESSION 1

Participant Response

Facilitator Response

SESSION 2

Participant Response

Facilitator Response

SESSION 3
Participant Response

Facilitator Response

SESSION 4
Participant Response

Facilitator Response

Tricky Tasks Challenge Sheet

Photocopy this sheet so that half your participants (those playing the parent role) will have one of the items after each is cut out. Notice there are two of each item. (You will have enough for 20 pairs.) Cut the items apart so they can be passed out as slips of paper to parent role-players.

Stand up and sing the first line of the National Anthem.	**Stand up and sing the first line of the National Anthem.**
Slap your legs with both hands, clap your hands together, then touch your hands to the top of your head.	**Slap your legs with both hands, clap your hands together, then touch your hands to the top of your head.**
Go to the facilitator and shake his/her hand; then go back to your seat and sit down.	**Go to the facilitator and shake his/her hand; then go back to your seat and sit down.**
Hop like a bunny rabbit three hops forward and three back.	**Hop like a bunny rabbit three hops forward and three back.**
Take your shoes off. (If they are already off, put them on.)	**Take your shoes off. (If they are already off, put them on.)**
Stand in the corner of the room that is farthest from here.	**Stand in the corner of the room that is farthest from here.**
Pretend you are crying.	**Pretend you are crying.**
Laugh hysterically.	**Laugh hysterically.**
Stand up, walk around your chair, clap your hands, and sit down.	**Stand up, walk around your chair, clap your hands, and sit down.**
Recite "Mary Had a Little Lamb."	**Recite "Mary Had a Little Lamb."**

Performance Learning Systems grants facilitator of this program the right to photocopy this page for use in group sessions.

Evaluation Form
for the *Being the Parent YOU Want to Be* Workshop

In order to provide future workshops that are meaningful and pertinent to your needs, we would appreciate your sincere responses to the following questions:

Facilitator:_____ Date:_____

Please rate the following:

	Excellent	Good	Fair	Poor
1. Usefulness of information and skills	☐	☐	☐	☐
2. Quality of leader	☐	☐	☐	☐
3. Preparation of leader	☐	☐	☐	☐
4. Organization of presentation	☐	☐	☐	☐
5. Overall effectiveness of workshop	☐	☐	☐	☐

How does this workshop compare with others you have taken?

☐ The best   ☐ Among the best   ☐ Comparable to others

☐ Not as good   ☐ Haven't taken others

This workshop has increased my understanding of:

I would be interested in other parenting workshops on the following topics:

1. _____   3. _____

2. _____   4. _____

Other comments:

Worksheet 1
My Perceived Parenting Style

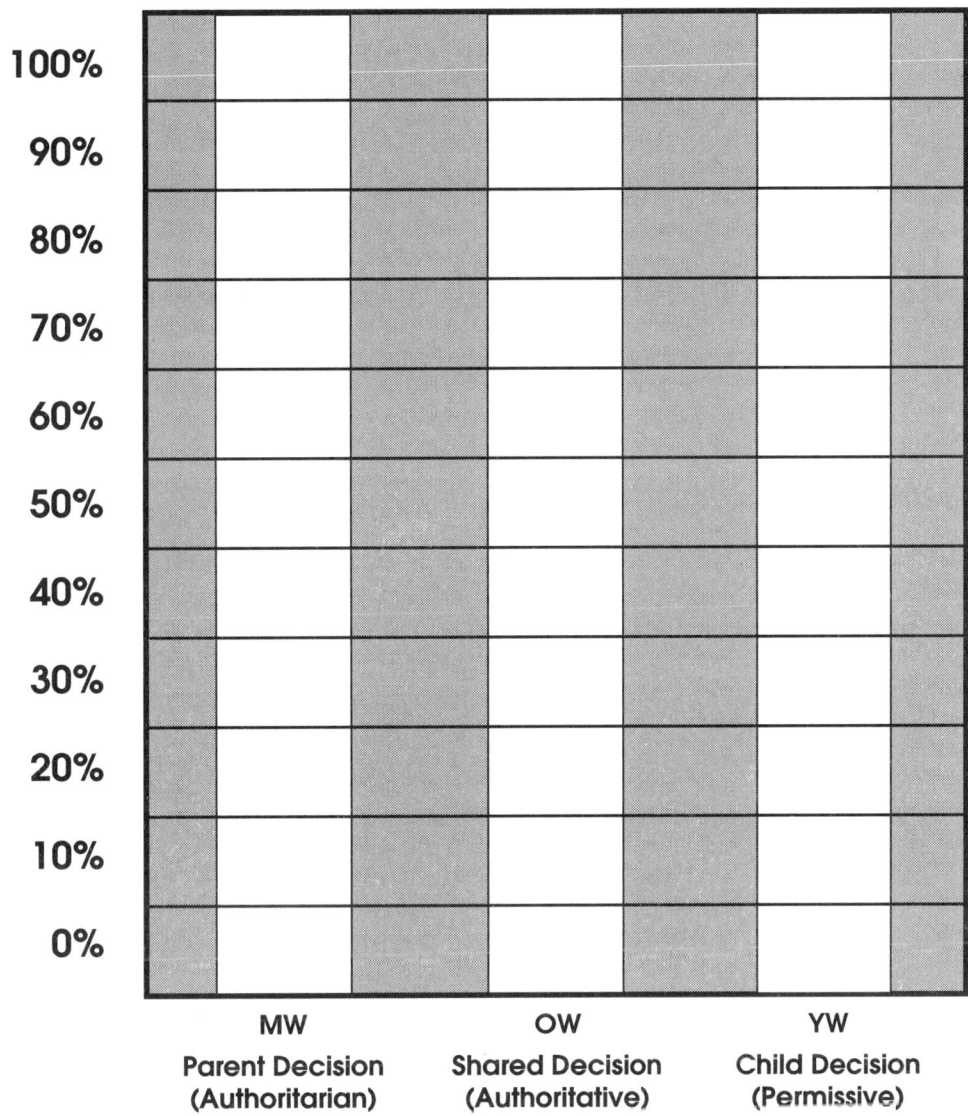

	MW	OW	YW
	Parent Decision (Authoritarian)	Shared Decision (Authoritative)	Child Decision (Permissive)

Note: MW + OW + YW should equal 100%

T-1

Appendix C
Sample Worksheet 1: My Perceived Parenting Style

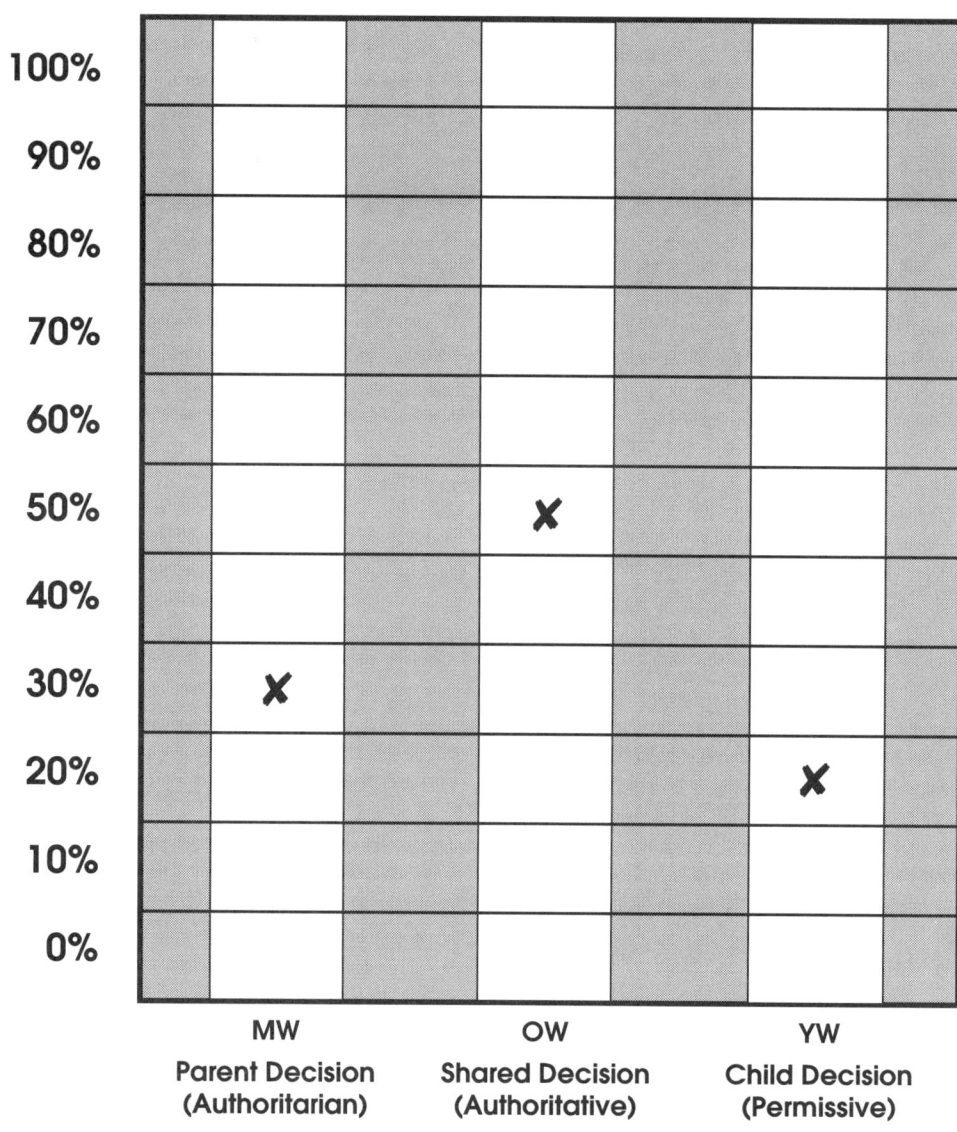

	MW	OW	YW
	Parent Decision **(Authoritarian)**	**Shared Decision** **(Authoritative)**	**Child Decision** **(Permissive)**

Note: MW + OW + YW should equal 100%

*These samples are actual responses from
one of the author's workshop participants.
This participant had two preschoolers.*

T-2

Worksheet 2
Who Decides?

Next to each statement below, show the percentage of time you:
1) Keep decision-making authority.
2) Share decision-making authority with your children.
3) Give decision-making authority to your children.

When added together, the three columns across each row should total 100%.

Example:

Who decides how to budget the family income?   85%   10%   5%

	MW Parent Decision	OW Shared Decision	YW Child Decision
1. Who decides what you will eat at mealtimes?			
2. Who chooses when and where your family will go for vacation?			
3. Who sets the rules for the way your children act at home?			
4. Who decides what happens when the kids break these rules?			
5. Who decides who will do which chores?			
6. Who picks your children's friends?			
7. Who decides what your family will do on your vacations?			
8. Who chooses your children's clothes and hairstyles?			
9. Who decides by what time your kids have to be home in the evening?			
10. Who sets bedtimes?			
Totals:			

T-3

Appendix D
Sample Worksheet 2: Who Decides?

Next to each statement below, show the percentage of time you:
1) Keep decision-making authority.
2) Share decision-making authority with your children.
3) Give decision-making authority to your children.

When added together, the three columns across each row should total 100%.

Example:

Who decides how to budget the family income?   85%   10%   5%

	MW Parent Decision	OW Shared Decision	YW Child Decision
1. Who decides what you will eat at mealtimes?	85%	10%	5%
2. Who chooses when and where your family will go for vacation?	60%	30%	10%
3. Who sets the rules for the way your children act at home?	50%	40%	10%
4. Who decides what happens when the kids break these rules?	90%	10%	0%
5. Who decides who will do which chores?	60%	30%	10%
6. Who picks your children's friends?	10%	10%	80%
7. Who decides what your family will do on your vacations?	20%	60%	20%
8. Who chooses your children's clothes and hairstyles?	10%	10%	80%
9. Who decides by what time your kids have to be home in the evening?	10%	80%	10%
10. Who sets bedtimes?	60%	30%	10%
Totals:	455	310	235

T-4

Worksheet 3
Factors in Decision Making

Next to each statement below, show the percentage of time you:
   1)   Keep decision-making authority.
   2)   Share decision-making authority with your children.
   3)   Give decision-making authority to your children.

When added together, the three columns across each row should total 100%.

   Example:
   The making of rules in our home is usally a: 70%   20%   10%

	MW Parent Decision	OW Shared Decision	YW Child Decision
1. My children would like more:			
2. Because of the age and maturity of my children, I tend more toward:			
3. Because of the problems I deal with, I favor:			
4. Because I am concerned about my children, I prefer:			
5. Because I work, or I am short of time, I prefer:			
6. Pressure from others, such as my husband/wife, influences me toward:			
7. The way friends treat their children makes me favor:			
8. How my parents raised me makes me want to use:			
9. If I didn't have to consider anything else, I would choose:			
10. Day-to-day I lean toward:			
Totals:			

Appendix E
Sample Worksheet 3: Factors in Decision Making

Next to each statement below, show the percentage of time you:
1) Keep decision-making authority.
2) Share decision-making authority with your children.
3) Give decision-making authority to your children.

When added together, the three columns across each row should total 100%.

Example:

	MW Parent Decision	OW Shared Decision	YW Child Decision
The making of rules in our home is usally a:	70%	20%	10%
1. My children would like more:	0%	10%	90%
2. Because of the age and maturity of my children, I tend more toward:	10%	50%	40%
3. Because of the problems I deal with, I favor:	10%	50%	40%
4. Because I am concerned about my children, I prefer:	50%	30%	20%
5. Because I work, or I am short of time, I prefer:	50%	30%	20%
6. Pressure from others, such as my husband/wife, influences me toward:	50%	30%	20%
7. The way friends treat their children makes me favor:	40%	30%	30%
8. How my parents raised me makes me want to use:	60%	30%	10%
9. If I didn't have to consider anything else, I would choose:	20%	60%	20%
10. Day-to-day I lean toward:	50%	30%	20%
Totals:	340	350	310

T-6

Worksheet 4A
Summary Table for Worksheets 2 and 3

	MW Parent Decision (Authoritarian)	OW Shared Decision (Authoritative)	YW Child Decision (Permissive)	Work- sheet Totals
Worksheet 2				
Worksheet 3				
Totals for Worksheets 2 and 3				
Divided by 2				
Divided by 10 (round off to nearest whole number and show as a percentage)				

T-7

Appendix F
Sample Worksheet 4A: Summary Table for Worksheets 2 and 3

	MW Parent Decision (Authoritarian)	OW Shared Decision (Authoritative)	YW Child Decision (Permissive)	Work-sheet Totals
Worksheet 2	455	310	235	1,000
Worksheet 3	340	350	310	1,000
Totals for Worksheets 2 and 3	795	660	545	2,000
Divided by 2	397.50	330	272.50	1,000
Divided by 10 (round off to nearest whole number and show as a percentage)	40%	33%	27%	100%

T-8

Worksheet 4B
My Actual Parenting Style

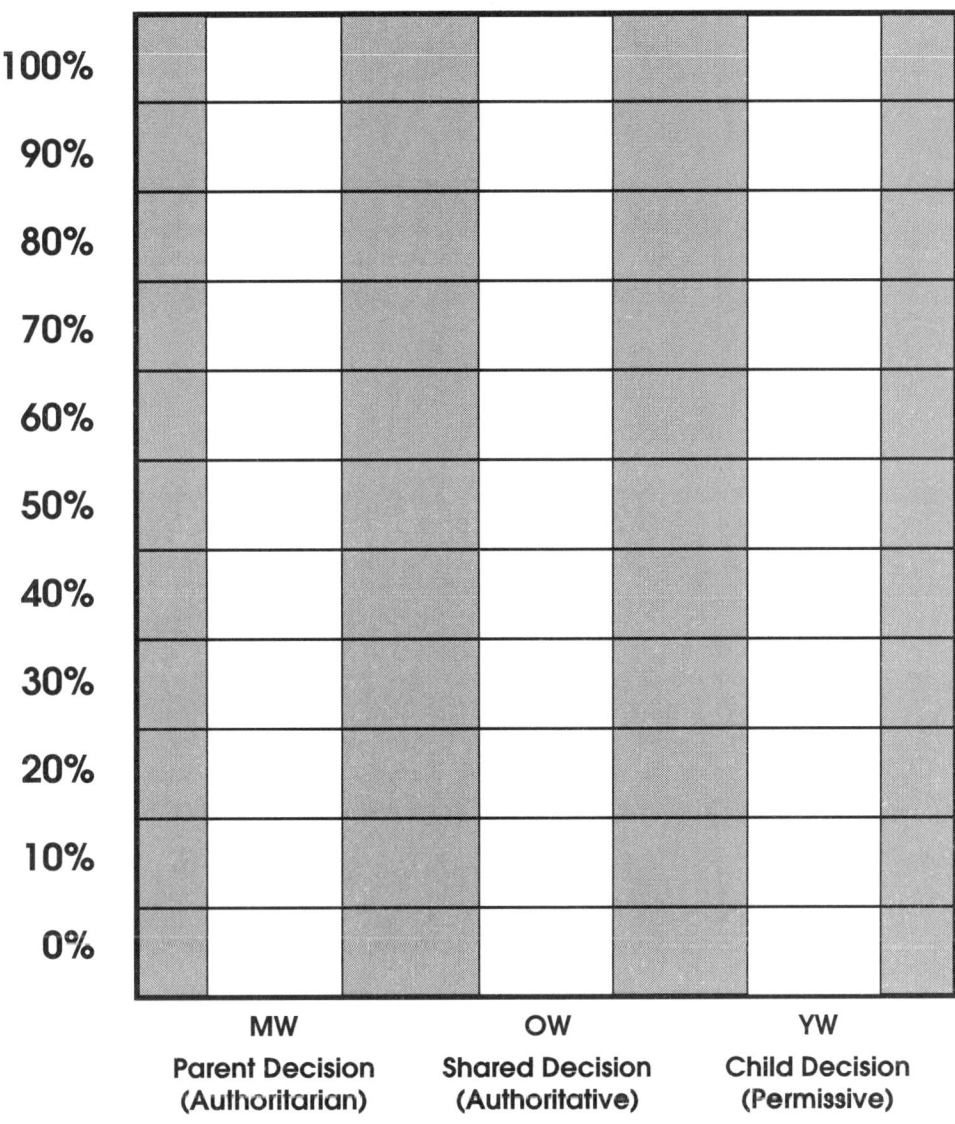

	MW	OW	YW
	Parent Decision (Authoritarian)	**Shared Decision (Authoritative)**	**Child Decision (Permissive)**

Note: MW + OW + YW should equal 100%

T-9

Appendix G
Sample Worksheet 4B: My Actual Parenting Style

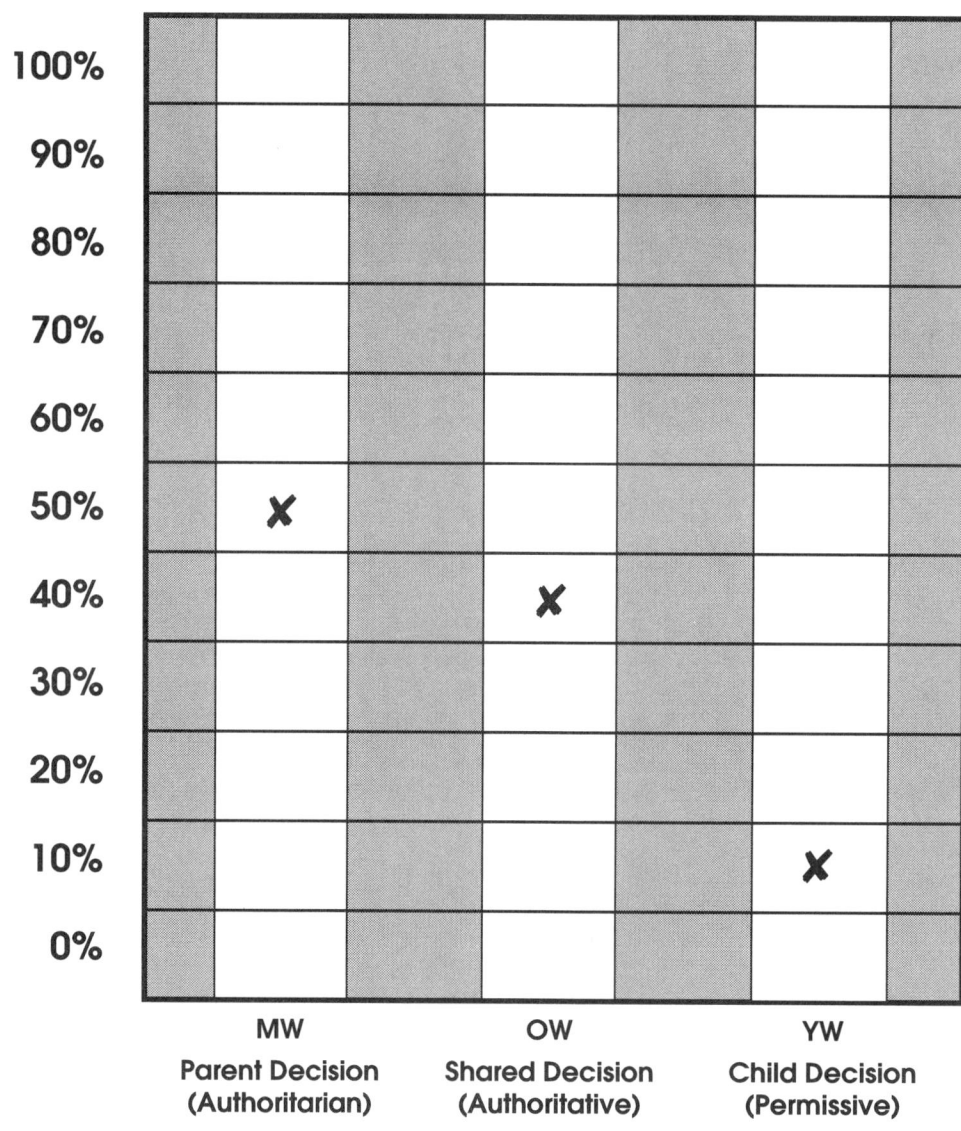

Note: MW + OW + YW should equal 100%

T-10

Worksheet 5
Are You Congruent?

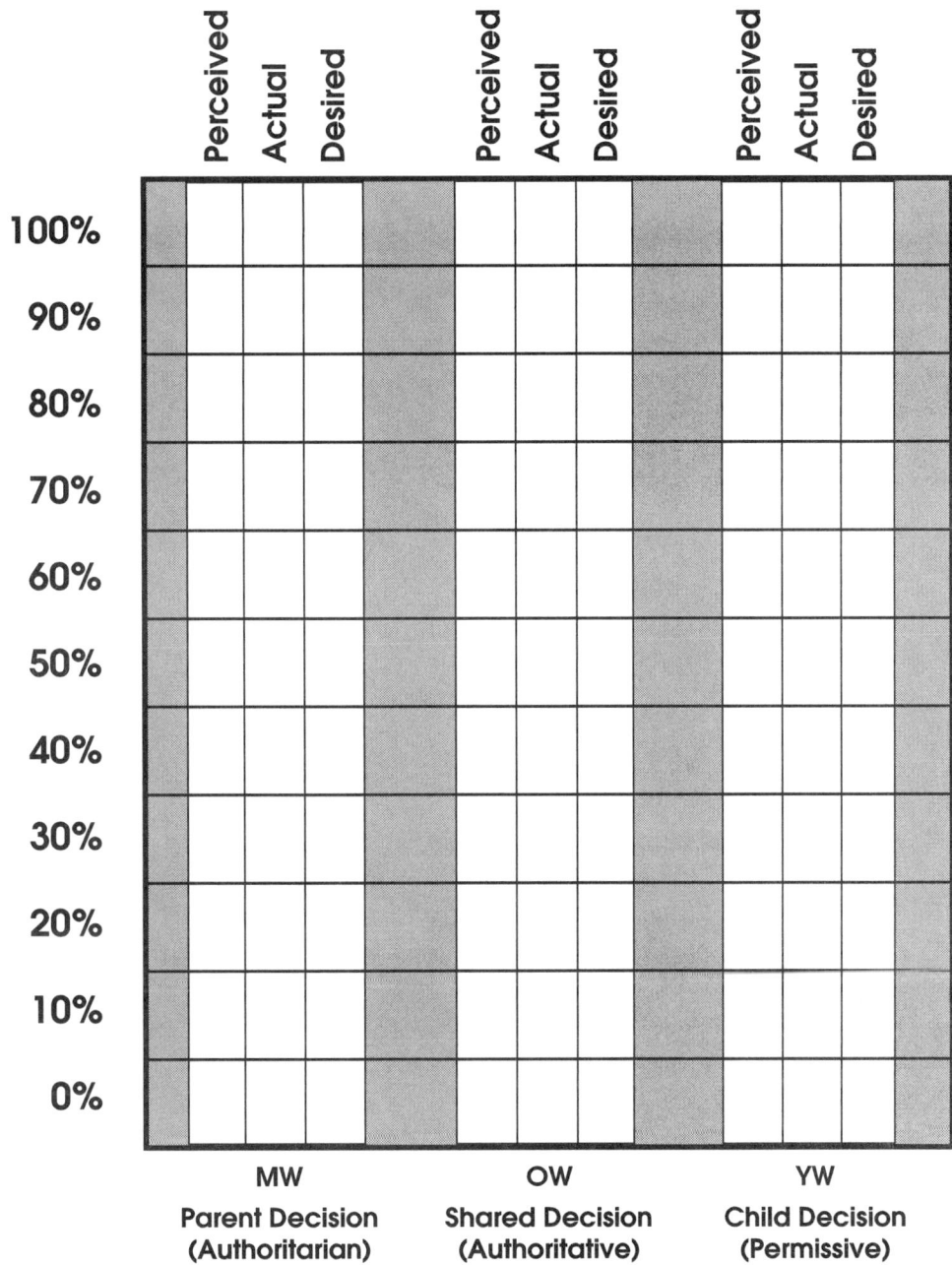

T-11

Appendix H
Sample Worksheet 5: Are You Congruent?

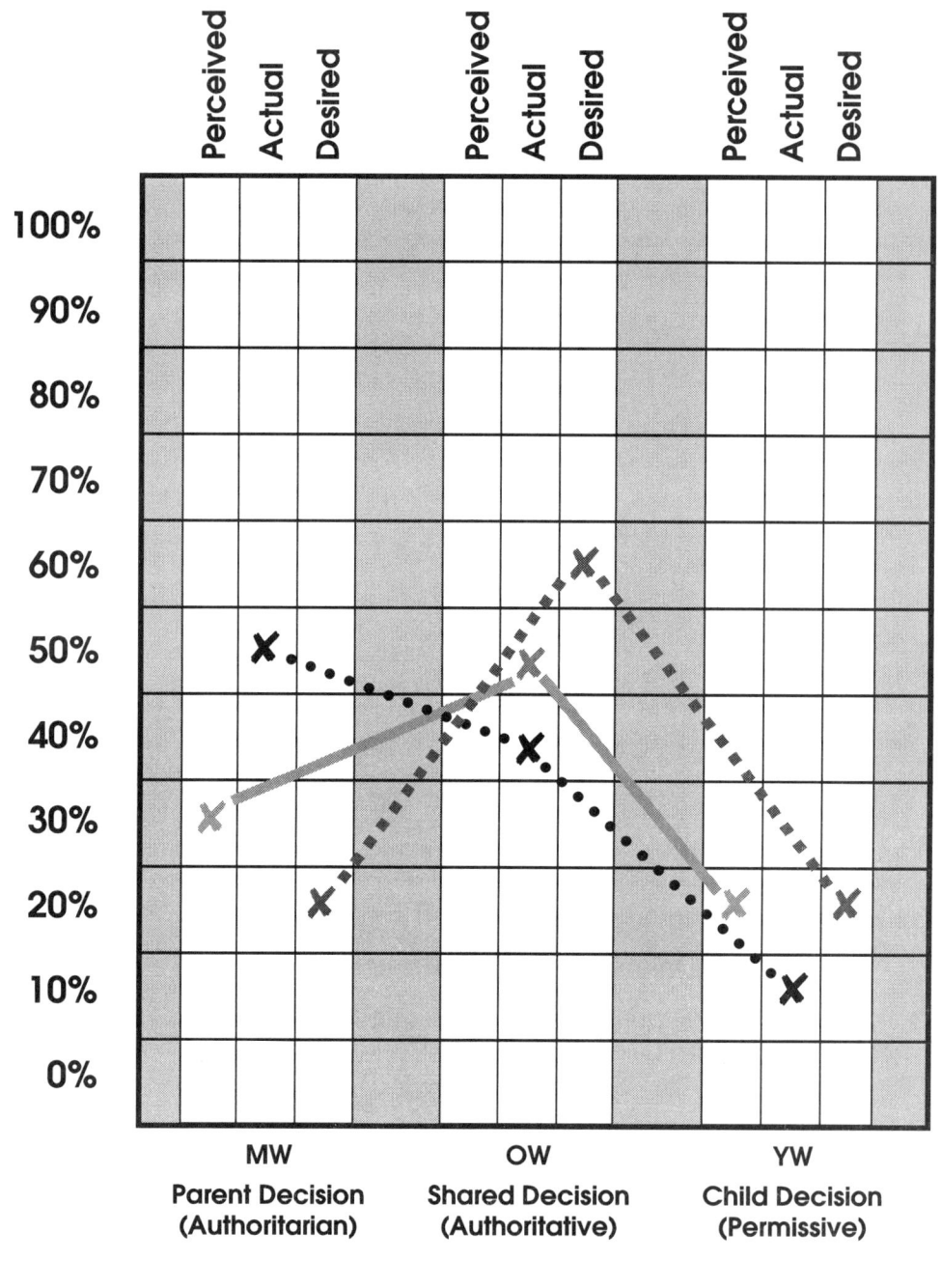

Key: ▬▬▬ **Perceived Parenting Style**   • • • **Actual Parenting Style**
      ■ ■ ■ **Desired Parenting Style**

T-12

Worksheet 6
Congruency Checkup

	No. of Observations	MW	Percentages OW	YW

**Skills for Discovering
What's On Your Child's Mind**

Tell-Me-What's-On-Your-Mind
Question ☐ ☐ ☐ ☐

Give-Me-Specific-Information
Question ☐ ☐ ☐ ☐

What-You-Meant Statement ☐ ☐ ☐ ☐

Think-It-Over Statement ☐ ☐ ☐ ☐

**Skills for Overcoming
Your Child's Objections**

Look-On-The-Bright-Side
Statement ☐ ☐ ☐ ☐

Walk-In-Their-Shoes Statement

  Pointed to success ☐ ☐ ☐ ☐

  Another direction ☐ ☐ ☐ ☐

Support-Their-Thinking Statement

  Total support ☐ ☐ ☐ ☐

  Gave additional information ☐ ☐ ☐ ☐

Catch-Them-Doing-It-Right
Statement ☐ ☐ ☐ ☐

**Skills for Solving Problems and
Making Decisions With Your Child**

Solve-The-Problem Question

  Asked for solutions:

    broad solutions ☐ ☐ ☐ ☐

    narrow solutions ☐ ☐ ☐ ☐

    very narrow solutions ☐ ☐ ☐ ☐

  Offered choices:

    equal choices ☐ ☐ ☐ ☐

    limited choices ☐ ☐ ☐ ☐

    Hobson's Choice ☐ ☐ ☐ ☐

This-Is-The-Deal Statement

  Parent acts first ☐ ☐ ☐ ☐

  Child acts first ☐ ☐ ☐ ☐

Out-Of-Bounds Statement ☐ ☐ ☐ ☐

Do-It-this-Way Statement ☐ ☐ ☐ ☐

Totals: MW + OW + YW = 100% ☐ ☐ ☐ ☐

T-13

Appendix I
Sample Worksheet 6: Congruency Checkup

(100 observations made)

	No. of Observations	MW	Percentages OW	YW
Skills for Discovering What's On Your Child's Mind				
Tell-Me-What's-On-Your-Mind Question	~~HHT~~ I		6%	
Give-Me-Specific-Information Question	~~HHT~~ IIII	9%		
What-You-Meant Statement	~~HHT~~			5%
Think-It-Over Statement	I		1%	
Skills for Overcoming Your Child's Objections				
Look-On-The-Bright-Side Statement	~~HHT~~ IIII			9%
Walk-In-Their-Shoes Statement				
Pointed to success	IIII		4%	
Another direction			0%	
Support-Their-Thinking Statement				
Total support	I		1%	
Gave additional information	~~HHT~~ II			7%
Catch-Them-Doing-It-Right Statement	~~HHT~~ II		7%	
Skills for Solving Problems and Making Decisions With Your Child				
Solve-The-Problem Question				
Asked for solutions:				
broad solutions	I		1%	
narrow solutions	~~HHT~~ II	7%		
very narrow solutions			0%	
Offered choices:				
equal choices	~~HHT~~ II		7%	
limited choices	~~HHT~~		5%	
Hobson's Choice	~~HHT~~ I	6%		
This-Is-The-Deal Statement				
Parent acts first	I		1%	
Child acts first	~~HHT~~ II	7%		
Out-Of-Bounds Statement	~~HHT~~ III	8%		
Do-It-this-Way Statement	~~HHT~~ IIII	9%		
Totals: MW + OW + YW = 100%	100	46%	33%	21%

T-14

Table 1
Range of Decision Making

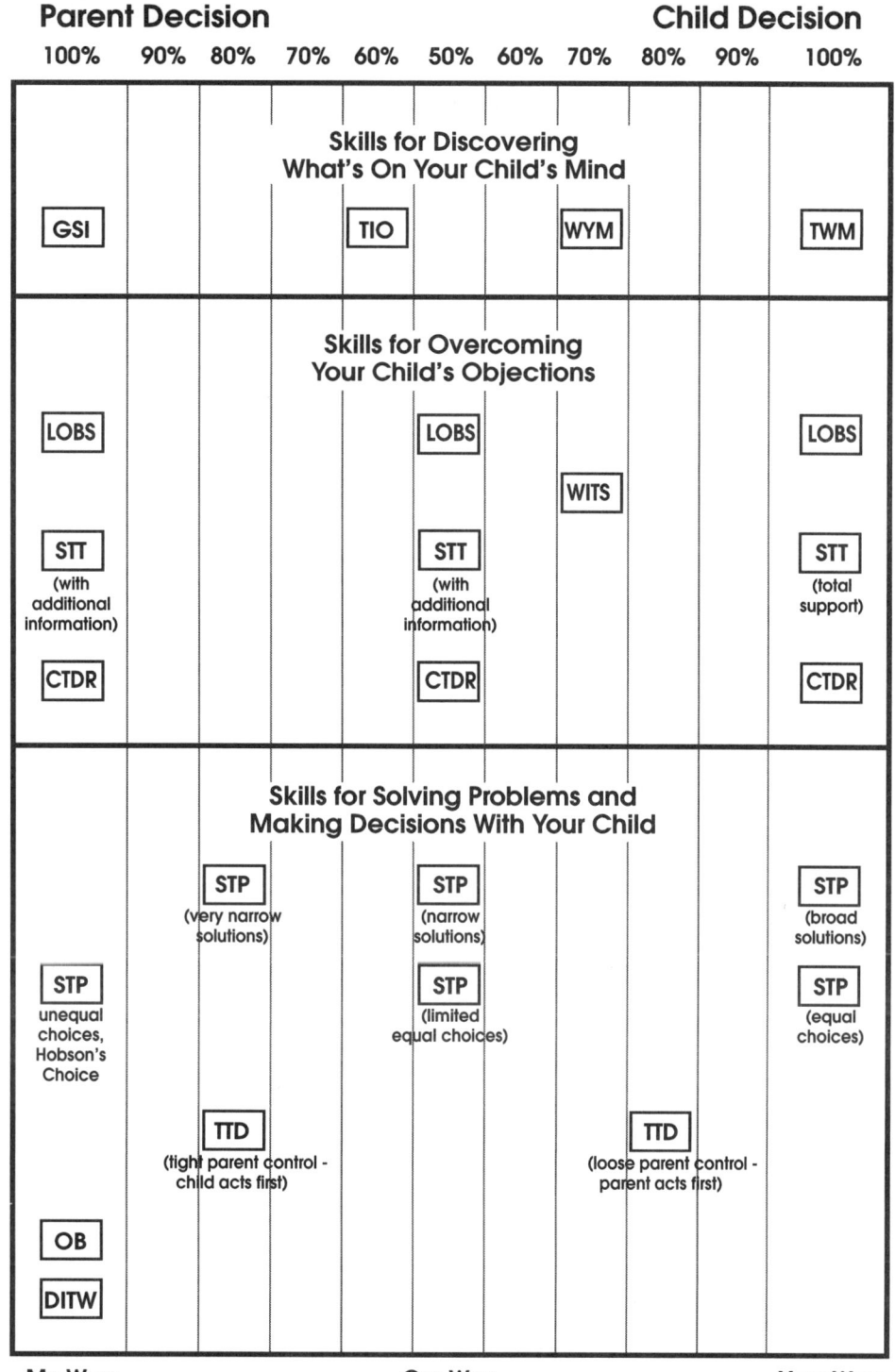

Parent Decision						Child Decision				
100%	90%	80%	70%	60%	50%	60%	70%	80%	90%	100%

Skills for Discovering What's On Your Child's Mind

GSI ... TIO ... WYM ... TWM

Skills for Overcoming Your Child's Objections

LOBS ... LOBS ... WITS ... LOBS

STT (with additional information) ... STT (with additional information) ... STT (total support)

CTDR ... CTDR ... CTDR

Skills for Solving Problems and Making Decisions With Your Child

STP (very narrow solutions) ... STP (narrow solutions) ... STP (broad solutions)

STP unequal choices, Hobson's Choice ... STP (limited equal choices) ... STP (equal choices)

TTD (tight parent control - child acts first) ... TTD (loose parent control - parent acts first)

OB

DITW

| My Way | Our Way | Your Way |

T-15

Appendix A

The 12 Communication Skills for Effective Parenting

Skills for Discovering What's On Your Child's Mind

1. Tell-Me-What's-On-Your-Mind Question (TWM)
2. Give-Me-Specific-Information Question (GSI)
3. What-You-Meant Statement (WYM)
4. Think-It-Over Statement (TIO)

Skills for Overcoming Your Child's Objections

5. Look-On-The-Bright-Side Statement (LOBS)
6. Walk-In-Their-Shoes Statement (WITS)
7. Support-Their-Thinking Statement (STT)
8. Catch-Them-Doing-It-Right Statement (CTDR)

Skills for Solving Problems and Making Decisions With Your Child

9. Solve-The-Problem Question (STP)
10. This-Is-The-Deal Statement (TTD)
11. Out-Of-Bounds Statement (OB)
12. Do-It-This-Way Statement (DITW)

T-16

Three Parenting Styles

"My Way" Parents
- Value obedience.
- Decide for children.
- Usually have young children.

"My Way" parents often make all the decisions and want instant obedience from their children. Parents of very young children often find themselves deciding for their children. This approach is called "keeping the power" (for the parents).

"Your Way" Parents
- Are permissive.
- Seldom demand much.
- Value children's independence.
- Let children decide.
- Rarely punish.
- Usually have older children.

"Your Way" parents are permissive. They demand little of their children. These parents let their children do their "own thing" as much as possible. Such parents do not control or punish. They often let very young children make decisions. This approach is called "giving the power" (to the children).

"Our Way" Parents
- Provide directions.
- Are flexible.
- Value give-and-take.

"Our way" parents get their authority from their knowledge and experience rather than from their position or power. These parents "share the power" of decision making with their children. They give clear, firm directions softened by reason and a give-and-take of ideas. As their children mature, these parents often share more of the decision-making power with their children.

T-17

"My Way" Parents

- Value obedience.

- Decide for children.

- Usually have young children.

"My Way" parents often make all the decisions and want instant obedience from their children. Parents of very young children often find themselves deciding for their children. This approach is called "keeping the power" (for the parents).

T-18

"Your Way" Parents

- Are permissive.

- Seldom demand much.

- Value children's independence.

- Let children decide.

- Rarely punish.

- Usually have older children.

"Your Way" parents let their children "do their own thing" as much as possible. These parents do not control. They often let even young children make decisions. This approach is called "giving the power" (to the children).

T-19

"Our Way" Parents

- Provide directions.

- Are flexible.

- Value give-and-take.

"Our Way" parents get their authority from their knowledge and experience rather than from their position or power. They "share the power" of decision making with their children. These parents give clear, firm directions softened by reason and a give-and-take of ideas. As their children mature, these parents often share more of the decision-making power with their children.

T-20

Tell-Me-What's-On-Your-Mind Question

- Gives children the freedom to speak.

- Addresses what the children think is important.

- Is often used with a "Your Way" parenting style.

Here's How

- "What do you think would have been the right way to do it?"

- "What will you do now?"

T-21

Give-Me-Specific-Information Question

- Limits children's answers to yes and no

  or

- Requests only what you want to know.

- Is often used with a "My Way" parenting style.

Here's How

- "Do you plan to share any of that with your brother?"

- "What do you need to take to school tomorrow?"

- "Which shirt do you want to wear?"

T-22

What-You-Meant Statement

Think positively!

Make a statement:
Restate the child's meaning.
Offer that meaning back to the child.

This is a "Your Way" parenting approach.

Here's How

- "You're hurt because she got the award."
(feeling)

- "You'll finish the job."
(intention)

- "You don't care how long it takes you."
(attitude)

T-23

Think-It-Over Statement

- Mentally identify the part of your child's thinking that doesn't make sense.

- Restate that part of your child's position that doesn't make sense.

- This is an "Our Way" parenting approach.

Here's How

- "Completing the work quickly is more important than having it look neat."

- "You expect to go out in the car tonight even though it is very foggy."

- "You are the only one whose parents said no."

T-24

Look-On-The-Bright-Side Statement

- Think positively.

- Tell children what you want them to do.

- All parenting styles use this skill.

Here's How

- "Hold the plates level when you carry them to the table."

- "Look left and right before you cross the street."

- "You can play your game when you have completed your work."

T-25

Walk-In-Their-Shoes Statement

- Let your children know you recognize and empathize with their feelings. Show them you understand. Perhaps talk about your own or another's experience.

- Refocus the child's attention:
  On a past or future success.
  In another direction.

- This is an "Our Way" parenting approach.

Here's How

- "It's frustrating to not get onto the cheerleading squad. Modern dance class starts tomorrow."

  (empathy, focus in another direction)

- "You seem disappointed with how much time it's taking you to learn the new computer program. Learning takes time. You'll get the hang of it. You've learned many other skills on the computer."

  (empathy, focus on past success)

T-26

Support-Their-Thinking Statement

- Children value their own opinions. Let your words and actions say, "I know you have your own reasons for believing as you do. I respect your point of view."

- Support children if you agree with them.

- Give them additional information to help them think more clearly if you disagree.

- All parenting styles use this statement.

Here's How

- "That's a great idea."   (total support)

- "You could take out the garbage later. The garbage service will be here in half an hour to empty the cans."   (additional information)

- "Going to an afternoon matinee sounds like a good idea. If you wait until evening, the rest of us can go too."   (additional information)

T-27

Catch-Them-Doing-It-Right Statement

- Show approval.

- Connect approval to a quality *the child* values.

- The two steps may be:
Given separately.
Combined into one statement.

- This is an "Our Way" parenting strategy. It is also useful with the "Your Way" style.

Here's How

- "I'm pleased with the way you two have been getting along. You've been very grown up."

  (two steps separately, children value maturity)

- "That was a smart thing you did, deciding not to make the purchase now."

  (steps combined, child values intelligence and wise decisions)

Performance Learning Systems grants facilitator of this program the right to photocopy this page for use in group sessions.

T-28

Solve-The-Problem Question

- State the problem.

- Ask for possible solutions allowing for:
  A broad range of solutions — "Your Way"
  A narrow range of solutions — "Our Way"
  A very narrow range of solutions — "My Way"

- Or offer choices:
  Equal — "Your Way"
  Limited — "Our Way"
  Unequal — "My Way"

Here's How

- "I have time Sunday. What would you like to do?"
  ("Your Way, broad range)

- "We can go to the mall for one pair of shoes.
  I can afford to spend no more than $50. What kind
  should we look for?"   ("Our Way," narrow range)

- "You may play video games for 30 minutes.
  There must be no shooting. Which game do you
  want to play?"   ("My Way," very narrow range)

- "You may get yourself into the bath or I will help
  you in."
  ("My Way," unequal choices, Hobson's Choice)

T-29

This-Is-The-Deal Statement

- Set up a contract with the child:

  Make a proposal about what one person will do (using the word "if" to begin the statement).

  Then state what is to be done by the other person in return.

  Whatever follows the word "if" must be done first.

- Since both parent and child must agree in order to make this work, it is an "Our Way" approach.

Here's How

- "If you'll wash the car now, I'll take you and your friends to the game."

  (requires the child to act first)

- "If I help you dust the living room now, you can help me sweep the porch."

  (requires the parent to act first)

Out-Of-Bounds Statement

- Determine what actions are unacceptable.

- Disapprove of the child's actions, not the child.

- This is a "My Way" parenting approach.

Here's How

- "Letting the neighbor's dog into our yard when your little sister is playing outside could cause her to get hurt."

- "Leaving the lights on in empty rooms runs up our electric bill."

- "Answering the phone without identifying yourself may confuse the caller."

- "Leaving your toys on the stairs could cause someone to trip and fall."

T-31

Do-It-This-Way Statement

- State what you want done.

- Give the reason.

- Either step:
  May come first.
  May be implied.

- Your statement will be correct if it tells the child why you want something done.

- This is a "My Way" parenting approach.

Here's How

- "Take your book bag. You will need what is in it."

- "Change your shirt. There is dirt on the front."

- "Turn off the hot water when your little brother is in the bathroom."   (reason implied)

T-32

Role-Play Observation Sheet for Discovering What's On Your Child's Mind

Case No. 1 — Parent role-player: _____

Remember to end the role-play after 20 minutes.

Skill Progression Chart

1. _____	11. _____	21. _____
2. _____	12. _____	22. _____
3. _____	13. _____	23. _____
4. _____	14. _____	24. _____
5. _____	15. _____	25. _____
6. _____	16. _____	26. _____
7. _____	17. _____	27. _____
8. _____	18. _____	28. _____
9. _____	19. _____	29. _____
10. _____	20. _____	30. _____

Abbreviations:

Tell-Me-What's-On-Your-Mind Question (TWM)

Give-Me-Specific-Information Question (GSI)

What-You-Meant Statement (WYM)

Think-It-Over Statement (IIO)

Comments:

T-33a

Role-Play Observation Sheet for Discovering What's On Your Child's Mind

Case No. 2 — Parent role-player: _____

Remember to end the role-play after 20 minutes.

Skill Progression Chart

1. _____	11. _____	21. _____
2. _____	12. _____	22. _____
3. _____	13. _____	23. _____
4. _____	14. _____	24. _____
5. _____	15. _____	25. _____
6. _____	16. _____	26. _____
7. _____	17. _____	27. _____
8. _____	18. _____	28. _____
9. _____	19. _____	29. _____
10. _____	20. _____	30. _____

Abbreviations:

Tell-Me-What's-On-Your-Mind Question (TWM)

Give-Me-Specific-Information Question (GSI)

What-You-Meant Statement (WYM)

Think-It-Over Statement (TIO)

Comments:

T-33b

Role-Play Observation Sheet for Discovering What's On Your Child's Mind

Case No. 3 — Parent role-player: _____

Remember to end the role-play after 20 minutes.

Skill Progression Chart

1. _____   11. _____   21. _____
2. _____   12. _____   22. _____
3. _____   13. _____   23. _____
4. _____   14. _____   24. _____
5. _____   15. _____   25. _____
6. _____   16. _____   26. _____
7. _____   17. _____   27. _____
8. _____   18. _____   28. _____
9. _____   19. _____   29. _____
10. _____   20. _____   30. _____

Abbreviations:

Tell-Me-What's-On-Your-Mind Question (TWM)

Give-Me-Specific-Information Question (GSI)

What-You-Meant Statement (WYM)

Think-It-Over Statement (TIO)

Comments:

Role-Play Observation Sheet for Overcoming Your Child's Objections

Case No. 1 — Parent role-player: _____

Remember to end the role-play after 20 minutes.

Skill Progression Chart

1. _____	11. _____	21. _____
2. _____	12. _____	22. _____
3. _____	13. _____	23. _____
4. _____	14. _____	24. _____
5. _____	15. _____	25. _____
6. _____	16. _____	26. _____
7. _____	17. _____	27. _____
8. _____	18. _____	28. _____
9. _____	19. _____	29. _____
10. _____	20. _____	30. _____

Abbreviations:

Tell-Me-What's-On-Your-Mind Question (TWM)

Give-Me-Specific-Information Question (GSI)

What-You-Meant Statement (WYM)

Think-It-Over Statement (TIO)

Look-On-The-Bright-Side Statement (LOBS)

Walk-In-Their-Shoes Statement (WITS)

Support-Their-Thinking Statement (STT)

Catch-Them-Doing-It-Right Statement (CTDR)

Comments:

T-34a

Role-Play Observation Sheet for Overcoming Your Child's Objections

Case No. 2 — Parent role-player: _____

Remember to end the role-play after 20 minutes.

Skill Progression Chart

1. _____	11. _____	21. _____
2. _____	12. _____	22. _____
3. _____	13. _____	23. _____
4. _____	14. _____	24. _____
5. _____	15. _____	25. _____
6. _____	16. _____	26. _____
7. _____	17. _____	27. _____
8. _____	18. _____	28. _____
9. _____	19. _____	29. _____
10. _____	20. _____	30. _____

Abbreviations:

Tell-Me-What's-On-Your-Mind Question (TWM)

Give-Me-Specific-Information Question (GSI)

What-You-Meant Statement (WYM)

Think-It-Over Statement (TIO)

Look-On-The-Bright-Side Statement (LOBS)

Walk-In-Their-Shoes Statement (WITS)

Support-Their-Thinking Statement (STT)

Catch-Them-Doing-It-Right Statement (CTDR)

Comments:

T-34b

Role-Play Observation Sheet for Overcoming Your Child's Objections

Case No. 3 — Parent role-player: _____

Remember to end the role-play after 20 minutes.

Skill Progression Chart

1. _____	11. _____	21. _____
2. _____	12. _____	22. _____
3. _____	13. _____	23. _____
4. _____	14. _____	24. _____
5. _____	15. _____	25. _____
6. _____	16. _____	26. _____
7. _____	17. _____	27. _____
8. _____	18. _____	28. _____
9. _____	19. _____	29. _____
10. _____	20. _____	30. _____

Abbreviations:

Tell-Me-What's-On-Your-Mind Question (TWM)

Give-Me-Specific-Information Question (GSI)

What-You-Meant Statement (WYM)

Think-It-Over Statement (TIO)

Look-On-The-Bright-Side Statement (LOBS)

Walk-In-Their-Shoes Statement (WITS)

Support-Their-Thinking Statement (STT)

Catch-Them-Doing-It-Right Statement (CTDR)

Comments:

T-34c

Role-Play Observation Sheet for Solving Problems and Making Decisions With Your Child

Case No. 1 — Parent role-player: _____

Remember to end the role-play after 20 minutes.

Skill Progression Chart

1. _____	11. _____	21. _____
2. _____	12. _____	22. _____
3. _____	13. _____	23. _____
4. _____	14. _____	24. _____
5. _____	15. _____	25. _____
6. _____	16. _____	26. _____
7. _____	17. _____	27. _____
8. _____	18. _____	28. _____
9. _____	19. _____	29. _____
10. _____	20. _____	30. _____

Abbreviations:

Tell-Me-What's-On-Your-Mind Question (TWM)

Give-Me-Specific-Information Question (GSI)

What-You-Meant Statement (WYM)

Think-It-Over Statement (TIO)

Look-On-The-Bright-Side Statement (LOBS)

Walk-In-Their-Shoes Statement (WITS)

Support-Their-Thinking Statement (STT)

Catch-Them-Doing-It-Right Statement (CTDR)

Solve-The-Problem Question (STP)

This-Is-The-Deal Statement (TTD)

Out-Of-Bounds Statement (OB)

Do-It-This-Way Statement (DITW)

Comments:

T-35a

Role-Play Observation Sheet for Solving Problems and Making Decisions With Your Child

Case No. 2 — Parent role-player: _____

Remember to end the role-play after 20 minutes.

Skill Progression Chart

1. _____	11. _____	21. _____
2. _____	12. _____	22. _____
3. _____	13. _____	23. _____
4. _____	14. _____	24. _____
5. _____	15. _____	25. _____
6. _____	16. _____	26. _____
7. _____	17. _____	27. _____
8. _____	18. _____	28. _____
9. _____	19. _____	29. _____
10. _____	20. _____	30. _____

Abbreviations:

Tell-Me-What's-On-Your-Mind Question (TWM)

Give-Me-Specific-Information Question (GSI)

What-You-Meant Statement (WYM)

Think-It-Over Statement (TIO)

Look-On-The-Bright-Side Statement (LOBS)

Walk-In-Their-Shoes Statement (WITS)

Support-Their-Thinking Statement (STT)

Catch-Them-Doing-It-Right Statement (CTDR)

Solve-The-Problem Question (STP)

This-Is-The-Deal Statement (TTD)

Out-Of-Bounds Statement (OB)

Do-It-This-Way Statement (DITW)

Comments:

T-35b

Role-Play Observation Sheet for Solving Problems and Making Decisions With Your Child

Case No. 3 — Parent role-player: _____

Remember to end the role-play after 20 minutes.

Skill Progression Chart

1. _____	11. _____	21. _____
2. _____	12. _____	22. _____
3. _____	13. _____	23. _____
4. _____	14. _____	24. _____
5. _____	15. _____	25. _____
6. _____	16. _____	26. _____
7. _____	17. _____	27. _____
8. _____	18. _____	28. _____
9. _____	19. _____	29. _____
10. _____	20. _____	30. _____

Abbreviations:

Tell-Me-What's-On-Your-Mind Question (TWM)

Give-Me-Specific-Information Question (GSI)

What-You-Meant Statement (WYM)

Think-It-Over Statement (TIO)

Look-On-The-Bright-Side Statement (LOBS)

Walk-In-Their-Shoes Statement (WITS)

Support-Their-Thinking Statement (STT)

Catch-Them-Doing-It-Right Statement (CTDR)

Solve-The-Problem Question (STP)

This-Is-The-Deal Statement (TTD)

Out-Of-Bounds Statement (OB)

Do-It-This-Way Statement (DITW)

Comments:

T-35c

ABOUT THE AUTHORS

GARY SCREATON PAGE

Gary Page is an award-winning teacher, school counselor, author, speaker, seminar/workshop facilitator, entrepreneur, and minister. For more than thirty-five years, he has taught students of all levels, from primary grades through college. During those years, he has worked with thousands of children and their parents.

He has been an educational consultant for children's television and has appeared on many national television and radio shows. He has developed parenting workshops based on the skills in his book and has helped countless families improve their communication skills.

Gary and his wife Rotraud are the parents of two grown children, Jason and Deidre, and grandparents of Austin and Kirsyn.

Gary is available for presentations to groups. Contact him through the PLS Speaker's Bureau at 800-757-3878.

CAROL ANN WEIR

Carol Ann Weir has been an educator for over thirty years, the last fourteen of which she has spent as an educational consultant and remediation specialist. During her career, she has amassed a wealth of experience not only in teaching but also in advising others on how to teach. She has given workshops for both educators and parents on subjects ranging from the 3 Rs to child psychology and has written a leader's guide for presenters of such workshops. She founded and operated her own school, teaching creative activities for preschool children and parenting techniques for their parents.

She has also been an educational consultant for a children's television series. Throughout her career, she has been a professional colleague and personal friend of Gary Page.

Her most valuable experience, however, has been as wife of Ron and mother of four grown children, Andrew, Michelle, Deborah, and Stephen.